Miranda v. Arizona

The Rights of the Accused

by John Hogrogian

FAMOUS
TRIALS

Lucent Books, San Diego, CA

Titles in the Famous Trials series include:

The Boston Massacre
Brown v. Board of Education
The Dred Scott Decision
Miranda v. Arizona
The Nuremberg Trials
The O.J. Simpson Trial
Roe v. Wade

The Salem Witch Trials
The Scopes Trial
The Trial of Adolf Eichmann
The Trial of Joan of Arc
The Trial of John Brown
The Trial of Socrates

Library of Congress Cataloging-in-Publication Data

Hogrogian, John.
    Miranda v. Arizona / by John Hogrogian.
        p. cm. — (Famous trials)
    Includes bibliographical references and index.
    Summary: Discusses the trial Miranda v. Arizona, including the crime, the state appeal, the Supreme Court decision, and its lasting effects.
    ISBN 1-56006-471-4 (lib. bdg. : alk. paper)
    1.Miranda, Ernesto—Trials, litigation, etc.—Juvenile literature. 2. Right to counsel—United States—Juvenile literature. 3. Confession (Law)—United States—Juvenile literature. 4. Police questioning—United States—Juvenile literature. [1. Miranda, Ernesto—Trials, litigation, etc. 2. Right to counsel. 3. Police questioning. 4. Civil rights—History.] I. Title. II. Title: Miranda versus Arizona. III. Series.
KF224.M54H64   1999
345.73'056—dc21   98-50357
                                                                    CIP
                                                                    AC

Table of Contents

Foreword

"The law is not an end in and of itself, nor does it provide ends. It is preeminently a means to serve what we think is right."

William J. Brennan Jr.

THE CONCEPT OF JUSTICE AND THE RULE OF LAW are hallmarks of Western civilization, manifested perhaps most visibly in widely famous and dramatic court trials. These trials include such important and memorable personages as the ancient Greek philosopher Socrates, who was accused and convicted of corrupting the minds of his society's youth in 399 B.C.; the French maiden and military leader Joan of Arc, accused and convicted of heresy against the church in 1431; to former football star O.J. Simpson, acquitted of double murder in 1995. These and other well-known and controversial trials constitute the most public, and therefore most familiar, demonstrations of a Western legal tradition that dates back through the ages. Although no one is certain when the first law code appeared or when the first formal court trials were held, Babylonian ruler Hammurabi introduced the first known law code in about 1760 B.C. It remains unclear how this code was administered, and no records of specific trials have survived. What is clear, however, is that humans have always sought to govern behavior and define actions in terms of law.

Almost all societies have made laws and prosecuted people for going against those laws, but the question of which behaviors to sanction and which to censure has always been controversial and remains in flux. Some, such as Roman orator and legislator Cicero, argue that laws are simply applications of universal standards. Cicero believed that humanity would agree on what constituted illegal behavior and that human laws were a mere extension of natural laws. "True law is right reason in agreement with nature," he wrote, world-wide in scope, unchanging, everlasting. . . . We may not oppose or alter that law, we cannot abolish it, we cannot be freed from its obligations by any legislature. . . . This [natural] law does not differ for Rome and for Athens, for the present and for the future. . . . It is and will be valid for all nations and all times.

Cicero's rather optimistic view has been contradicted throughout history, however. For every law made to preserve harmony and set universal standards of behavior, another has been born of fear, prejudice, greed, desire for power, and a host of other motives. History is replete with individuals defying and fighting to change such laws—and even to topple governments that dictate such laws. Abolitionists fought against slavery, civil rights leaders fought for equal rights, millions throughout the world have fought for independence—these constitute a minimum of reasons for which people have sought to overturn laws that they believed to be wrong or unjust. In opposition to Cicero, then, many others, such as eighteenth-century English poet and philosopher William Godwin, believe humans must be constantly vigilant against bad laws. As Godwin said in 1793:

Laws we sometimes call the wisdom of our ancestors. But this is a strange imposition. It was as frequently the dictate of their passion, of timidity, jealousy, a monopolizing spirit, and a lust of power that knew no bounds. Are we not obliged perpetually to renew and remodel this misnamed wisdom of our ancestors? To correct it by a detection of their ignorance, and a censure of their intolerance?

Lucent Books' *Famous Trials* series showcases trials that exemplify both society's praiseworthy condemnation of universally unacceptable behavior, and its misguided persecution of individuals based on fear and ignorance, as well as trials that leave open the question of whether justice has been done. Each volume begins by setting the scene and providing a historical context to show how society's mores influence the trial process and the verdict.

Each book goes on to present a detailed and lively account of the trial, including liberal use of primary source material such as direct testimony, lawyers' summations, and contemporary and modern commentary. In addition, sidebars throughout the text create a broader context by presenting illuminating details about important points of law, information on key personalities, and important distinctions related to civil, federal, and criminal procedures. Thus, all of the primary and secondary source material included in both the text and the sidebars demonstrates to readers the sources and methods historians use to derive information and conclusions about such events.

Lastly, each *Famous Trials* volume includes one or more of the following comprehensive tools that motivate readers to pursue further reading and research. A timeline allows readers to see the scope of the trial at a glance, annotated bibliographies provide both sources for further research and a thorough list of works consulted, a glossary helps students with unfamiliar words and concepts, and a comprehensive index permits quick scanning of the book as a whole.

The insight of Oliver Wendell Holmes Jr., distinguished Supreme Court justice, exemplifies the theme of the *Famous Trials* series. Taken from *The Common Law*, published in 1881, Holmes remarked: "The life of the law has not been logic, it has been experience." That "experience" consists mainly in how laws are applied in society and challenged in the courts, a process resulting in differing outcomes from one generation to the next. Thus, the *Famous Trials* series encourages readers to examine trials within a broader historical and social context.

Introduction

"No person . . . shall be compelled in any criminal case to be a witness against himself."
—Fifth Amendment to the U.S. Constitution

"[N]or shall any State deprive any person of life, liberty, or property, without due process of law."
—Fourteenth Amendment to the U. S. Constitution

"It is a fair summary of history to say that the safeguards of liberty have frequently been forged in controversies involving not very nice people."
—Justice Felix Frankfurter in a dissenting opinion in the 1950 U.S. Supreme Court decision of *United States v. Rabinowitz*

ERNESTO MIRANDA STOOD TRIAL in the Arizona Superior Court in Phoenix on June 2, 1963. He faced charges of rape and kidnapping. There was no publicity about the trial in the media, and few, if any, people sat in the courtroom to watch the testimony. By all appearances, it was just another case arising out of the increasing amount of violent crime in American cities of the 1960s. The jury quickly found Miranda guilty, and the judge gave him a long prison sentence.

On appeal, however, some very dedicated and able lawyers used Miranda's case, along with three other cases, as a vehicle to bring some very important legal issues before the U.S. Supreme Court. The issues were about police interrogation of criminal suspects in their custody. Before the 1960s, the police really had only one restriction when they questioned suspects. They could not compel suspects to confess by threatening them with violence, beating them, or depriving them of food or sleep. Other forms of pressure or trickery were allowed, and the confessions that resulted could be used against those suspects in criminal trials.

In the 1960s, the Supreme Court was paying close attention to the criminal justice systems of the states. Under the leadership of Chief Justice Earl Warren, the Supreme Court took a first look at police interrogation practices in a 1964 case, but it made its most complete declaration about interrogation in Ernesto Miranda's case and its three companion cases.

In its 1966 decision in the four cases, the Supreme Court held that the police must give certain warnings to criminal suspects before they interrogate them. The Court wanted suspects to know that they do not have to answer police questions, and it wanted to prevent the police from obtaining confessions from people who are ignorant of their right to

Supreme Court chief justice Earl Warren presided over the hearing of arguments in Miranda v. Arizona.

remain silent. One part of the warning required by the Court is that the suspect has the right to remain silent and that any statement can be used against him or her in a trial. The Supreme Court for the first time was requiring the police to tell suspects about these rights before any interrogation took place.

The Supreme Court also required the police to tell suspects before interrogation that they have the right to have an attorney with them during questioning. Another part of the warning required by the Court is that the suspect is entitled to a lawyer appointed and paid by the government if he or she cannot afford to hire a private lawyer. Finally, the Supreme Court decision required the police to prove that a suspect freely gave up his or her rights if he or she confessed without an attorney present.

Public opinion was divided on the wisdom and the legal correctness of the Supreme Court decision. Some thought that the Court had done well to protect the rights of all people in police custody, especially poor people and racial and ethnic minorities. Others thought that the Court had made it easier for criminals to get away with their crimes and to return to the streets to hurt more victims. Some people agreed with the Supreme Court that what became known as the Miranda warnings were the only practical way to make sure every American, whether educated in the law or not, knew of his or her right to remain silent as guaranteed by the Fifth Amendment to the Constitution. Others thought that the Supreme Court was improperly imposing its views of criminal justice on the states without any basis in the Constitution.

A young man bends over as a police officer handcuffs him. The Miranda *ruling made it mandatory for officers to inform suspects of their legal rights upon arrest.*

Richard Nixon greets Texan supporters during his 1968 presidential campaign. During the campaign Nixon criticized the Supreme Court's stance on criminal defendants' rights.

The debate over suspects' rights inevitably spilled over into politics. Richard Nixon made "law and order" a central theme of his presidential campaigns in 1968 and 1972. He freely criticized the criminal law decisions of the Supreme Court under Chief Justice Warren as being too protective of the rights of criminals. After he was elected, President Nixon appointed Chief Justice Warren Burger to replace Earl Warren in 1969; since then, all the members of the Court that decided *Miranda* have retired and been replaced. The principles of *Miranda*, however, have remained in effect to this day. The case of Ernesto Miranda is an important story of law and politics in the last half of the twentieth century. Its importance is likely to continue for many years to come.

Chapter 1

The Crime

MIRANDA V. ARIZONA WAS A rape case. Rape is a crime in which one person (usually a male) forces another person (usually a female) into having sexual relations when she does not want to. The victim was Lois Ann Jameson (to protect her privacy, this is not her real name). She was an eighteen-year-old who lived in the northeast section of Phoenix, Arizona. She lived with her mother, her older sister, and her sister's husband. She was a shy young woman who had dropped out of school. She had a job working at the concession stand at the Paramount Theater in downtown Phoenix.

On Saturday night, March 2, 1963, Lois Ann was at work in the Paramount, selling refreshments to the moviegoers. The feature film that day was *The Longest Day*, a movie about the D-Day invasion of France during World War II. The last showing of the film ended at about 11:15 P.M. After finishing her work for the day, she stayed in the theater until about 11:30, chatting with a young man who also worked there.

At about 11:30, Lois Ann and her coworker walked together to the corner of Seventh Street and Monroe Street, two blocks away from the theater. They waited together for a bus that would take them from downtown to the northeast section of Phoenix. At about 11:45, the bus came. Both Lois Ann and her coworker climbed aboard.

After about a twenty-five-minute ride, Lois Ann got off the bus at the corner of Seventh Street and Marlette Street, the stop nearest her home. Her coworker stayed on the bus. It was now about ten minutes after midnight on Sunday morning, March 3. Lois Ann started walking east on Marlette Street. It was dark, and there were no other people around. Her home was only a few blocks away on Citrus Way, and she regularly walked this route on her way home from work.

Kidnapped on the Way Home

The routine nature of the evening changed suddenly when a car pulled out of a driveway near the bus stop and then parked at the curb on the same block. A man got out of the car and walked in her direction. Lois Ann didn't think that there was anything suspicious about the stranger as she continued walking. As he passed her, however, the man suddenly grabbed Lois Ann around the middle with one arm and put his other hand over her mouth. The man told the frightened Lois Ann, "If you don't scream, I won't hurt you."[1] The hand over her mouth silenced her pleas to be let go. The man pulled her toward his car, opened the back door, and shoved her into the backseat. He tied her ankles together with a piece of rope and then tied her wrists together behind her back with more rope. Lois Ann was too shocked and scared to scream or struggle. The man put her down in the backseat, held a sharp object (which felt like a knife) to her throat, and told her not to move. Lois Ann began sobbing, and the man got into the driver's seat and started the car.

The man drove for about twenty or twenty-five minutes. He made a few turns but basically headed east. Lying across the backseat, Lois Ann did not scream during the drive. She remembered the man's warning. When the man pulled the car over, they were in the desert area to the east of Phoenix. The

A cactus grows in the desert outside of Phoenix, Arizona, near the site where the rape of Lois Ann Jameson occurred.

The car in which Ernesto Miranda raped Lois Ann Jameson was later found parked outside his home by police detectives.

man got out of the car and stayed outside of it for ten minutes. Lois Ann was helpless, arms and legs tied together with rope, unable to leave the backseat of the car. Although there was no gag over her mouth, she remained silent. She feared the man who had captured her from the street. In any case, there was nobody in the desert to hear any screams.

The Crime in the Desert

Finally, the man opened the back door and got in. He untied Lois Ann's arms and legs and told her to sit up. He told her to take her clothes off. She refused, so he removed her clothes and underclothes, leaving her wearing only her shoes. He then pushed her back down onto the backseat in a prone position, but she did not put up a physical struggle. The man was bigger and stronger than she was, and she believed that he had a knife. He ignored her cries and pleas to be released.

Sitting beside Lois Ann in the backseat, the man removed his pants and underpants. He left his T-shirt on. "You can't tell me you have never done this before," he said to the terrified young woman. "No, I haven't,"[2] Lois Ann screamed. Her protests made no difference. The man lay down on top of her. While she pushed him away with her hands, he forcibly and clumsily had sexual intercourse with Lois Ann.

After he had completed the act, the man opened the door and got out of the car. He put his clothing back on and then got into the driver's seat. He told Lois Ann to get dressed. For five minutes, she just lay on the backseat and cried, but she finally sat up and put her clothing on. While she dressed, the man asked her for money. She gave him the $4 that she had in her purse. He then ordered her to lie down on the backseat, facing the seat back. He drove her back to the northeast section of Phoenix, the neighborhood in which Lois Ann lived. On the way, the man said, "Whether you tell your mother what has happened or not is none of my business, but pray for me." [3]

At about 1:30 in the morning, the man pulled the car to the curb at 12th Street and Rose Lane, about four blocks from Lois Ann's home. She got out of the car, and the man drove off. She walked one block, then began running home, crying as she went.

Notifying the Police

Lois Ann pounded on the front door of her home. Her older sister Sarah (also not her real name) opened the door and let her in. Lois Ann was crying, her hair was disheveled, and the new suit that she had worn to work was a mess. For about fifteen minutes, Lois Ann cried, but she would not tell her sister what had happened. When she finally became calm enough to tell Sarah what had happened, Sarah immediately called the police.

At 2:08 A.M. in the early hours of Sunday, a police officer came to Lois Ann's home in response to the phone call made by her sister just a short time before. Lois Ann told the police officer about what had happened to her that night. He listened to her and then drove her to Good Samaritan Hospital for a medical examination. Such examinations are necessary in rape cases to both treat any injuries to the victim and gather evidence about the crime.

Once the doctor had finished with the medical examination, two police detectives interviewed Lois Ann at the hospital. She told them that she had struggled hard to fight the man off. She described the rapist as a Mexican man, about twenty-seven or twenty-eight years old, about 5'11" tall, about 175 pounds in weight, with short black, curly hair and dark-rimmed glasses. She said that he must not have shaved that day, as he had whiskers on his face. She did not notice any accent, scars, tattoos, or special identifying marks. She did not know who her attacker was.

Lois Ann also told the detectives about the car the man drove, describing it as an older green car. On the inside, the car had smelled like paint or turpentine. She noticed one peculiar thing about the car: A piece of rope was fastened to the rear of the car's front seat, apparently so that people in the backseat could grab it and pull themselves forward when getting out of the car. The rope was something that the car's owner had installed, not a piece of equipment installed by the manufacturer.

The Day After the Crime

Lois Ann went home and got some rest. Later that Sunday morning, however, a police officer came to her home and asked her to come with him to police headquarters, where detectives

THE CARE OF RAPE VICTIMS

When Lois Ann Jameson was raped in 1963, the care that rape victims received was not as good as it is today. Although doctors at that time would treat the physical injuries suffered in the attack, not as much was done for the emotional injuries that rape can cause.

It is important for a rape victim to get quick medical attention. A doctor can treat any injuries that the victim may have received during the attack. Hospital staff can test the victim for any sexually transmitted diseases and can take steps to prevent pregnancy. Important evidence is also collected during the medical examination and treatment in hospital emergency rooms. Doctors can recover samples of bodily fluids and hairs that can help identify the rapist and contribute to his conviction at trial. For this reason, a rape victim should not change her clothes or bathe after the crime until she has had the medical examination.

In today's society, more resources are available to help rape victims and their loved ones recover from the emotional injuries caused by the crime. Rape crisis centers, located in almost all large cities, offer help to victims and their families. With time and care, rape victims can recover from the emotional injuries that rape inflicts.

again asked Lois Ann about the attack. Two parts of her story puzzled the detectives. First, since Lois Ann had said that she physically resisted the attack, the detectives wondered why she had no bruises or rope marks on her body. Second, Lois Ann had said that, until the attack, she had been a virgin—that is, she had never had sexual intercourse before. However, the doctor who wrote the report believed from his examination that Lois Ann had not been a virgin. He had not found any sign of bleeding, which often happens when a woman has sexual intercourse for the first time.

The detectives told Lois Ann that these discrepancies in her story raised some doubts about whether she was telling the truth about the attack. Lois Ann said that she indeed had told the truth. The detectives asked if she would take a lie-detector test, technically known as a polygraph test, and Lois Ann agreed. The detectives said that they would schedule a test for later in the week.

The detectives then drove Lois Ann home. On the way, she pointed to a 1955 Chevrolet and said that the rapist's car was similar.

Detective Cooley Begins His Investigation

On Monday, March 4, the Phoenix Police Department assigned Detective Carroll Cooley to the case. After reading the paperwork that had been produced about the case so far, Detective Cooley drove to Lois Ann's home to discuss the case. Lois Ann had gone to work at the theater, but her sister discussed the case with the detective. She told him that Lois Ann was a shy and naive young woman. She said that Lois Ann had been taught not to resist an attacker physically, that it was better to submit rather than risk a beating or other life-threatening injury. Sarah said that that might explain the absence of bruises and scrapes on Lois Ann's body. Sarah also said that Lois Ann certainly had been a virgin before the attack and that the doctor who thought otherwise was mistaken. Detective Cooley then drove downtown to the Paramount Theater. He met Lois Ann and agreed to interview her the next day when she was not at work.

On Tuesday, March 5, Detective Cooley picked Lois Ann up at her home and drove her down to police headquarters. They discussed the attack in detail. She told the same story again but admitted that she had not put up a physical struggle against the rapist. She went on to say that, because of embarrassment, she had said in her previous statements that she had struggled. Detective Cooley also asked her about the route that the rapist had followed in driving to the desert, but she was unable to give him any information about that. Lois Ann also looked through books of photographs, known as mug shots, of all known white and Mexican sex offenders in the Phoenix area. She did not recognize anyone in the books.

The case did not advance any on Wednesday. On Thursday, March 7, Detective Cooley drove Lois Ann to police headquarters to take her polygraph test. The results were inconclusive, meaning that it was not possible to say for certain whether Lois Ann was telling the truth. Detective Cooley dropped Lois Ann at home and then drove back downtown, where he visited the Paramount Theater. He interviewed the young man who worked with Lois Ann and who had taken the bus with her on Saturday night. He confirmed the facts of the bus trip, but he could not help in identifying the rapist.

The Lucky Break in the Investigation

No further progress was made on Friday and Saturday, but on Saturday night at about 11:45, Lois Ann's brother-in-law Josh (not his real name) was walking from their home on Citrus Way to the bus stop at the corner of Seventh Street and Marlette Street. Ever since the attack, he made a habit of meeting Lois Ann at that corner when she got off the bus on the way back from work. On his way to the corner on Saturday, he noticed that an old Packard automobile was slowly driving around the streets near the bus stop. He wrote down what he thought was that car's license plate number: DFL-312. He went to the corner and waited until the bus came and Lois Ann got off. Together they began walking home. On the way, Josh saw the same car, which was now parked on the street. He and Lois Ann walked toward the car to look at it, but it suddenly raced away as they neared. Lois Ann said that it looked very similar to the car the rapist had driven.

On Monday, March 11, Josh called Detective Cooley and told him what had happened Saturday night. He gave the detective the license plate number and told him that the car he had seen looked like a 1953 Packard. Detective Cooley and Detective Wilfred Young checked the automobile registration records and found that DFL-312 was assigned to a new Oldsmobile. They realized that Josh might have seen the plate numbers incorrectly because of the dark, so they checked other plates that began with DFL. The registration records showed that DFL-317 was assigned to a 1953 Packard owned by Twila N. Hoffman of Mesa, a suburb outside Phoenix. After nine days, the police finally had a promising lead to follow.

On Tuesday, March 12, the two detectives went to the Mesa address of Twila Hoffman. They were surprised to find that no one lived in the house. When they spoke to a neighbor, they learned that Hoffman and the young Mexican man who lived with her had moved out of the house over the past weekend. The neighbor said that the young man's name was Ernesto Miranda and that he worked for United Produce in Phoenix. Police records showed that Miranda had been convicted in the past of several crimes, one of which was assault with intent to commit rape. When the detectives visited United Produce, the company confirmed that he worked there on the loading dock at night. They did not have his new address.

On Wednesday, March 13, Detectives Cooley and Young got Miranda's new address from the post office: He had told the post office to forward his mail to 2525 West Mariposa in Phoenix. When the detectives went to 2525 West Mariposa at about 9:00 A.M., a 1953 green Packard was parked outside. When the detectives looked inside a rear window, they saw a piece of rope attached to the rear of the front seat. Lois Ann had mentioned just such a piece of rope when describing the rapist's car to them. The detectives were confident that they were close to solving the crime.

Taking Miranda into Custody

The detectives knocked on the front door of the house. Twila Hoffman answered the door. They asked for Mr. Miranda, and Hoffman went to wake him up. After having worked all night at United Produce, he had gone to bed only about an hour before. The detectives asked him to come to police headquarters to discuss a case that they were investigating. Miranda went along with the officers. As he said later, "I didn't know whether I had a choice."[4]

LINEUPS

When the police find a suspect that they believe committed a crime, they need to have the victim identify the suspect (if possible) as the criminal. Human memory is not perfect, and a crime victim may have been so upset during the attack that he or she cannot remember what the attacker looked like. Honest police do not want to show a suspect to an uncertain victim in a way that suggests that the suspect is the attacker. A victim in that situation may accept the suggestion and identify the suspect as the attacker despite no independent memory of the attacker's appearance. Such suggestive identification procedures can lead to conviction of innocent people.

In a proper lineup, the suspect stands in a line with other people who look somewhat the same as he or she does. All the people in the line (including the suspect) should be the same approximate height, weight, and age. They should also have the same general clothing and hairstyle. If the lineup is not suggestive and the victim does pick out the suspect, that is strong evidence that the suspect committed the act. Even under perfect conditions, how-

During a police lineup a participant speaks into a microphone.

ever, a victim can sometimes identify the wrong person as the criminal. Because of that, the police need to work hard to develop other evidence to build their case.

At police headquarters, the detectives arranged for Lois Ann Jameson to view a lineup. In a lineup, the police put several persons in a row and ask a crime victim or witness whether he or she recognizes any of the people in the line as the person who committed the crime. The usual procedure is for the victim or witness to view the lineup from behind a one-way mirror so that the people in the line cannot see or hear the victim or witness. In Lois Ann's case, the police arranged a line of four young Mexican men, all similar in height, hair, and casual dress. Miranda wore a sign around his neck reading "1." The other men were prisoners from the Phoenix city jail, not suspects, and they wore signs marked 2, 3, and 4.

Lois Ann came to police headquarters in the late morning and looked at the lineup through the one-way mirror. She told the detectives that she could not identify any of the four men as

Ernesto Miranda (far left) and three jail inmates participate in a lineup at the Phoenix police headquarters on March 13, 1963.

Statistics About Rape

Most rape victims are raped by someone they know, such as friends, acquaintances, or family members. Almost half of all rapes take place in the victim's home or the rapist's home, with only about one-fifth of rapes taking place outdoors and another one-fifth in cars. Lois Ann Jameson's case was not the typical rape case because she was attacked in the street by a total stranger. In two other senses, she was typical because a majority of rape victims are eighteen years of age or younger and because between 90 and 95 percent of rape victims are female.

More than 50 percent of rapes are never reported to the police. One reason is that the victim often knows the rapist and fears further violence by him. Another reason is that the victim may be embarrassed because of the sexual nature of the crime. Many accused rapists go free at trial because there are usually no witnesses to the crime. That is why it is important to have evidence collected at a medical examination as soon as possible after the attack.

her attacker. She did say that number 1 had a build and facial features similar to those of her rapist. The detectives were disappointed but not discouraged by Lois Ann's inability to recognize number 1 as her attacker. After the lineup was over, Detectives Cooley and Young escorted Miranda into interrogation room number two.

Chapter 2

The Interrogation and Confession

THERE WERE NO CAMERAS or tape recorders present when Ernesto Miranda sat down with Detectives Cooley and Young behind the closed door of interrogation room number two in the police headquarters in Phoenix on March 13, 1963. They were in the room for about two hours, from about 11:30 A.M. to about 1:30 P.M. On the morning of March 14, the *Arizona Republic* (a daily newspaper in Phoenix) printed a story about what came out of that meeting. The headline on the story read "Man Signs Confession":

> A 23-year-old Phoenix produce worker arrested yesterday admitted being involved in attacks on three young Phoenix women, police reported.
>
> Police said Ernest Arthur Miranda of 2525 W. Mariposa has signed a statement confessing the rape of an 18-year-old girl, the attempted rape and robbery of a 23-year-old woman, and the accosting and robbery of another teenage girl.
>
> The 18-year-old victim said on March 3 the suspect forced her into a car as she walked from a bus stop to her west side home. She said he held a knife at the side of her neck.[5]

The newspaper used the English form of Miranda's name (Ernest Arthur), which the police used in the court papers instead of the Spanish name his parents had given him (Ernesto

Arturo). The newspaper article went on to say that Miranda had confessed to forcing his way into a twenty-three-year-old woman's car in November 1962, trying to rape her, and fleeing with $8 taken from her when she resisted his attack. The article also said that he had confessed to approaching a car in a parking lot on February 22, 1963, threatening the eighteen-year-old woman driver with a knife, and fleeing when she screamed and another car came onto the scene. The article reported that the parking-lot victim "supplied police with a description of tattooed initials 'E.M.' which eventually led police to Miranda." The article further stated that "police said he has such marks on his right hand."[6]

In the two-hour interrogation, Miranda had confessed to three crimes. The most serious of those crimes was his rape of Lois Ann Jameson. Miranda faced the likelihood of a long prison sentence, so why did he confess?

Detectives Cooley and Young generally described what happened in interrogation room number two. When Miranda asked about the lineup he had just stood in, one of the detectives said "you flunked."[7] The detectives told Miranda that Lois Ann had picked him out of the lineup as her attacker, even though, in reality, Lois Ann had not been able to identify him with any certainty. At the start of the interrogation, Miranda falsely believed that the victim had already identified him.

According to the two detectives, they did not threaten or strike Miranda during the interrogation. They also said that they made no promises to him of any lenient treatment in return for a confession. They said that they only asked him questions about the three crimes, primarily about the rape. There is no record of what questions were asked or of what evidence the detectives claimed to have against him. Late in the interrogation, a police officer brought Lois Ann to interrogation room number two. One of the detectives asked Miranda, "Is that the girl?" Miranda replied, "That's the girl."[8]

The detectives asked Miranda to write out his confession. He wrote his confession about the rape on a police form that had printed near its top the statement, "I make this statement

Miranda signed this form after his two-hour-long interrogation, confessing to the kidnapping and rape of Jameson.

voluntarily and of my own free will, with no threats, coercion, or promises of immunity, and with full knowledge of my legal rights, understanding any statement I make may be used against me." He described the crime as follows:

Seen a girl walking up street. Stopped a little ahead of her. Got out of car. Walked towards her. Grabbed her by the arm and asked to get in the car. Got in car without force. Tied hands & ankles. Drove away for a few miles. Stopped. Asked to take clothes off. Did not, asked me to take her back home. I started to take clothes off her without any force, and with cooperation. Asked her to lay down and she did. Could not get penis into vagina. Got about 1/2 (half) inch in. Told her to get clothes back on. Drove her home. I couldn't say I was sorry for what I had done. But asked her to say a prayer for me.[9]

The poorly educated Miranda left most of the periods and capital letters out of the statement. Although he denied using force, he admitted to grabbing Lois Ann on the street, tying her up, and having sexual intercourse with her after she had refused to do so. His confession was powerful evidence that he had raped Lois Ann.

Miranda later described the interrogation, emphasizing his fear and fatigue:

Once they get you in a little room and they start badgering you one way or the other, "you better tell us . . . or we're going to throw the book at you" . . . that is what was told to me. They would throw the book at me. They would try to give me all the time they could. They thought there was even the possibility that there was something wrong with me. They would try to help me, get me medical care if I needed it. . . . And I haven't had any sleep since the day before. I'm tired. I just got off work, and they have me and they are interrogating me. They mention first one crime, then another one, they are certain I am the person . . . knowing what a penitentiary is like, a person has to be frightened, scared. And not knowing if he'll be able to get back up and go home.[10]

However fearful or fatigued he might have been, Ernesto Miranda had nevertheless signed a confession that was likely to send him to prison for a large part of his life.

THE RIGHT TO APPOINTED COUNSEL

In 1963 not all states provided attorneys to represent poor criminal defendants the way Arizona did in Miranda's case. On March 18, 1963, however, only three days after Miranda's arraignment, the U.S. Supreme Court issued its decision in *Gideon v. Wainwright.* Clarence Earl Gideon had been charged with breaking into a closed pool room in Panama City, Florida, and stealing some money, wine, and cigarettes. Unable to hire an attorney, Gideon asked the judge to appoint a lawyer to represent him. The judge refused, and the jury found Gideon guilty after a trial in which he had no attorney. The case eventually reached the Supreme Court, which appointed prominent attorney (and future member of the Court) Abe Fortas to represent him. The Court ruled unanimously that the due process clause of the Fourteenth Amendment to the Constitution requires courts in all states to appoint a lawyer to represent a poor criminal defendant at trial if he or she is facing the possibility of a prison sentence of one year or more. The *Gideon* decision did not address the issue of whether the state had to appoint an attorney to advise poor criminal suspects at the time of police interrogation. The *Miranda* case would ultimately resolve that issue.

Clarence Earl Gideon's appeal to the Supreme Court resulted in a landmark ruling.

Ernesto Miranda Gets an Attorney

After he confessed on Wednesday afternoon, Miranda was held for the rest of the day and overnight in a city jail cell. On Thursday morning, he appeared briefly before a city magistrate and was transferred to the larger county jail. On Friday morning, March 15, he was arraigned before a justice of the peace in the Justice Court for the Northeast Phoenix Precinct. Arraignment is a court appearance at which a person accused of a crime receives formal written notice of the charges against him.

In the criminal complaint, dated March 14, 1963, Miranda was accused of the two crimes of kidnapping and rape in the first degree because of his acts against Lois Ann Jameson in the early morning hours of March 3. Another criminal complaint charged him with the robbery of $8 from a woman in November 1962.

The justice of the peace assigned a lawyer to represent Miranda in both cases and scheduled his rape trial for May 14, about two months away, in the superior court in Phoenix. Serious crimes were tried in the superior court, a higher court than the justice court. State law in Arizona required each county to provide a lawyer for anyone accused of a crime who did not have enough money to hire a lawyer. Miranda did not have enough money to hire a lawyer, so the justice of the peace appointed Alvin Moore to represent him. Moore was a seventy-three-year-old attorney with more than forty years of experience in his profession. In the 1920s and 1930s, he had tried many criminal cases in the courts of Oklahoma. He had practiced law in Phoenix since 1951, although his practice generally did not include criminal trials. For representing Miranda at trial, Moore received $100 from Maricopa County, far less than an attorney would charge a private client. Moore did not need the money; he took appointed criminal cases as a matter of civic duty.

The Insanity Defense

Alvin Moore interviewed Miranda and began to plan his defense. The confession made things look bad for the accused. Moore decided to argue to the superior court that Miranda was insane and that he should be committed to a mental hospital, rather than be convicted of a crime. On May 13, 1963, one day before the scheduled rape trial, Moore filed with the court a legal document that stated "COMES NOW, the defendant, ERNEST ARTHUR MIRANDA, and shows the Court that he intends to show evidence at the time of the trial of each of the above numbered and styled cases [the rape case and the robbery case], that he was insane at the time of the commission of the

THE INSANITY DEFENSE

The document Alvin Moore, Miranda's first attorney, filed with the superior court raised the issue of insanity in two different ways. First, he argued that Miranda was mentally ill, and because of this mental illness, he should not be held criminally responsible for his attack on Lois Ann Jameson. Under Arizona law, a defendant could not be held criminally responsible if the defendant did not know what he or she was doing or did not know the act was wrong. The judge usually allows the jury to determine whether the defendant was so insane at the time of the act that he or she cannot be found guilty. A defendant found not guilty by reason of insanity will not be convicted of the crime but will be committed to a mental hospital until the doctors there feel that there is no chance that he or she will commit another act of that nature.

Moore's document also claimed that Miranda was incompetent to stand trial. In every state, a defendant cannot be put on trial for a crime if he or she, because of mental illness, cannot understand the nature of the trial or assist his or her attorney in defending the case. If the judge finds a person incompetent to stand trial, the defendant is hospitalized until he or she is judged well enough to stand trial.

---

offenses and that he is insane or mentally defective at the time of the trial of said causes." [11] The court responded to this document by postponing the robbery trial until June 18 and the rape trial until June 19 and appointing two psychiatrists to examine Miranda at the jail.

Dr. Leo Rubinow met with Miranda on May 22 and June 4. In his written report to the superior court, he stated that Miranda was psychologically immature and unstable and "is unable to control his sexual impulses and drives." The doctor concluded, however, that "at neither interview was there any evidence of any psychotic manifestations noted or elicited, nor history of any psychotic episodes obtained." [12] In other words, Dr. Rubinow found that Miranda had psychological problems, but he was not insane in the sense that he could not tell right from wrong or could not understand the nature of the criminal charges against him.

Dr. James Kilgore met with Miranda on May 26. In the report he submitted to the superior court (in which he misspelled Miranda's name), Dr. Kilgore reached the same conclusion as had Dr. Rubinow. "It is my opinion that Mr. Mirande is aware of the charges that have been brought against him and is able to co-operate with his attorney in his own defense. Although Mr. Mirande has an emotional illness, I feel that at the time the acts were committed that he was aware of the nature and quality of the acts and that he was further aware that what he did was wrong." [13] Although Dr. Kilgore stated that Miranda suffered from a form of schizophrenia, he found that he was not so insane that he did not know his acts were wrong.

On June 18, 1963, the superior court ruled, as expected, that Miranda was not insane at the time he assaulted Lois Ann Jameson. The robbery trial was scheduled for the next day, June 19. The rape trial was scheduled for the day after, June 20.

Ernesto Miranda's Troubled Youth

This was not the first time Ernesto Miranda had faced criminal trouble in his twenty-three years of life. He was born in Mesa, Arizona, in 1940. He was the youngest of five children, all boys. When he was six years old, his mother died. His father remarried a year later, but young Ernesto did not get along well with his stepmother. He attended a Catholic grammar school in Mesa, where he often skipped school and was a disciplinary problem when he did show up. At age thirteen, he graduated from the eighth grade. He started high school but dropped out in his freshman year.

In 1954, the same year in which he finished eighth grade, Ernesto was arrested for auto theft. A court found him guilty and placed him on probation, meaning that he was allowed to go free as long as he stayed out of trouble. Unfortunately for young Ernesto, he was found guilty of burglary in 1955 and was sent to the state reform school for juvenile delinquents. He was re-leased after six months. Shortly after his release, he was found guilty of assault and attempted rape. He went back to the reform school for a year.

When he left the reform school in 1957, Ernesto was still only sixteen years old. He moved by himself to Los Angeles, California, where he supported himself by working in a grocery

THE BILL OF RIGHTS

When the thirteen colonies declared their independence from Great Britain in 1776, most of them adopted new constitutions that included a bill of rights, which is a statement of basic individual rights and liberties that government must respect. In 1781, eleven of these original states ratified the new U.S. Constitution, creating our federal government. The new Constitution did not have a bill of rights, and several ratifying states called for one to be added so that the federal government would not threaten some liberties held dear by Americans.

In March 1789, Congress met for the first time in New York City. James Madison, a member of the House of Representatives from Virginia and a future president of the United States, proposed that the Constitution be amended by adding a bill of rights. After debating and revising the proposal, both the Senate and the House of Representatives adopted the Bill of Rights. By December 1791, enough states ratified the Bill of Rights to make it a part of the Constitution.

The Bill of Rights consists of the first ten amendments to the Constitution. The Fifth Amendment contains several protections for defendants in federal criminal trials, including the provision that no person "shall be compelled in any criminal case to be a witness against himself." American political leaders knew that English authorities had used torture as late as the 1600s to extract confessions from criminal suspects, religious dissenters, and political opponents. They also knew that English criminal suspects had been expected to answer, under oath, all questions relating to the crime at issue, including those about their own participation. The leaders of the new American republic made sure that under the Constitution, as amended by the Bill of Rights, federal officials had to respect the decision of suspects to stay silent under questioning. Courts would eventually decide whether Ernesto Miranda's confession under Phoenix police questioning complied with the requirements of the Bill of Rights.

store. He was arrested for peeping into people's windows and spent three days in jail. He was also arrested twice for armed robbery, but he was not convicted of those crimes.

In April 1958, now seventeen years old, Ernesto joined the army. He was stationed at Fort Campbell in Kentucky, where he continued to get into trouble. He was in the army for fifteen months and spent six of those months in the stockade, which is a military jail. He was again found guilty of peeping into people's windows, and he was also absent without leave (commonly known as AWOL) for a time. Finally, the army gave him an undesirable discharge in July 1959.

Prison and a Fresh Start

After being discharged from the army, the eighteen-year-old Ernesto drifted from Kentucky to Tennessee to Arizona. In August 1959, he spent two weeks in jail in Texas for vagrancy. In December 1959, his troubles got worse. He was arrested for driving a stolen car. He was convicted of the crime and sentenced to one year and one day in prison. Ernesto began his sentence in a federal penitentiary in Ohio. In May 1960, he was transferred to a federal prison in California at his own request, saying that he wanted to be closer to his family in Arizona.

Ernesto was released from prison in January 1961. With little education and a criminal record, Ernesto did not have bright prospects. He was not close with any of his family members. It seems his luck had changed, however, when he met twenty-eight-year-old Twila Hoffman, a married woman who had two children but was separated from her husband. Ernesto and Twila fell in love, and he moved in with her and her children in California. In 1962, they had a new baby daughter. They decided to move to his hometown of Mesa, Arizona. She supported the family of five by working at a nursery school. He had a hard time keeping a job at first, but in August 1962, he started work at United Produce in Phoenix. He liked the work, and his supervisors liked him.

Miranda's life had been going well, but now he was about to go to trial on serious criminal charges.

Chapter 3

The Trial

O N WEDNESDAY, JUNE 19, 1963, Ernesto Miranda appeared before Judge Yale McFate of the Arizona Superior Court in Phoenix. He was tried for the robbery charge that had been brought against him. In criminal trials, the prosecutor presents evidence that will show that the accused (officially called "the defendant") is guilty of the charges. If the defendant has confessed to the charged crime, the prosecutor can show the confession to the jury as evidence of guilt. Before it can find the accused guilty, a jury must find beyond a reasonable doubt that the accused had committed all the acts charged. The defense attorney (representing the defendant) seeks to convince the jury that there is a reasonable doubt about the defendant's guilt; the primary tools are cross-examination of the prosecutor's witnesses and presenting the testimony of witnesses favorable to the defendant.

In Miranda's robbery trial, the prosecutor presented the testimony of the victim and a copy of his written confession. The trial lasted only a few hours, and the jury found Miranda to be guilty as charged. The judge postponed sentencing until June 27.

On the next day, Thursday, June 20, Miranda was again before Judge McFate, this time for his trial of the charges of kidnapping and raping Lois Ann Jameson; it would be this trial for which Ernesto Miranda became famous. This case would eventually go all the way to the U.S. Supreme Court in Washington, D.C., and would be debated for years to come by lawyers, politicians, and the public at large.

On that Thursday morning in 1963, however, *State v. Miranda* was just one of many criminal cases in the superior court and seemed no more noteworthy than any other case. Ernesto Miranda wore a brown suit and sat at the defense table with his attorney, Alvin Moore. At the prosecutor's table was Lawrence Turoff, a deputy county attorney for Maricopa County. A jury of twelve people (nine men and three women) sat in the jury box, a special seating area for the dozen people who listen to the witnesses, examine evidence, and then decide who is to be believed. These twelve jurors were a different group from the twelve who had been the jury for Miranda's robbery trial. When the trial began, this jury knew nothing about Ernesto Miranda or Lois Ann Jameson. Also present in the little courtroom were a stenographer to copy down everything that was said, a court clerk to help the judge keep track of witnesses and evidence, and a court officer to act as a security guard for the court.

In this artist's rendition, a jury forewoman reads the verdict during a criminal trial. Juries are responsible for weighing the evidence presented and reaching a verdict.

The first order of business in the morning was the prosecutor's presentation of his evidence against Miranda. Turoff presented the testimony of four witnesses: Lois Ann Jameson, her sister, Detective Cooley, and Detective Young. He would also present Miranda's written confession. This looked in advance to be a very strong case.

Moore had two strategies to defend Miranda. He would try to show that Lois Ann Jameson had agreed to have sexual intercourse with Miranda. He would also try to have the judge keep the jury from seeing the written confession because Miranda had been questioned without a lawyer to advise him.

The Victim's Testimony

The prosecution called Lois Ann Jameson as its first witness. She spoke in a very soft voice and at one point started to cry. Answering Turoff's questions, she told the jury how she had left work late on March 2 and had taken the bus to her neighborhood. She described getting off the bus and then seeing a car suddenly pull out of a parking lot and park on the street. She then testified as follows:

Q. What happened next, Lois Ann?

A. Well, I started walking and I noticed that this man was coming towards me.

Q. At that time, did you see where he came from?

A. Yes, from the parked car. I didn't see him get out of the car.

Q. All right, you saw a man walking towards you. What happened?

A. I didn't pay attention because I always pass people walking on that street, and I just kept on walking, and finally, well, I just—it happened so suddenly, I didn't have time to do anything.

Q. What happened?

A. Well, he told me not to scream, that he wouldn't hurt me.

Q. Did he touch you in any way?

A. Yes, he had my hands behind my back and one hand over my mouth and he started pulling me towards the car.[14]

Lois Ann then pointed at Miranda and said that he was the man who had attacked her.

Turoff continued his questioning:

Q. Now, after he grabbed you, Lois Ann, relate to us what happened next?

A. Well, he started pulling me toward the car and he put me in the back seat, and then he tied my hands and my ankles, and after he got out, he put this sharp thing to my neck and said, "Feel this."

Q. Did he say anything else?

A. No, that is all he said, and he got into the front seat and we drove for approximately twenty minutes.[15]

She then told of how Miranda drove to a secluded area outside Phoenix.

Lois Ann cried as she told the jury that Miranda took her clothes off. She said that she "didn't try to struggle because there was no place to run to." She then answered Turoff's questions about the rape:

A. After he undressed, he pushed my legs and got between them and then he was over me.

Q. He was over you; was he undressed at that time?

A. Yes.

Q. And you were undressed at that time?

A. Yes.

Q. What took place then, Lois Ann?

A. Well, he was over me, and I was undressed and he was undressed, and then he tried to make penetration.

Q. Did he make penetration?

A. At first, he didn't succeed, and then he sat—he waited for about five minutes, and then he started again.

Q. Did he succeed at that time?

A. Yes.[16]

Lois Ann stated that Miranda had engaged in sexual intercourse with her.

Turoff asked Lois Ann whether Miranda had forced her into intercourse against her will:

Q. Did you at any time, Lois Ann, permit him to do this voluntarily?

MR. MOORE: We object to the form of the question, leading and suggestive.

THE COURT: Overruled.

MR. TUROFF: You may answer. Did you permit him to do this voluntarily?

A. Well, he was a lot stronger than I was.

Q. Now, during the period of time that he made penetration, Lois Ann—strike that—what were you doing during this period of time that you have just testified to?

A. I was pushing against him with my hands. I kept screaming. I was trying to get away but he was a lot stronger than I was, and I couldn't do anything.[17]

Lois Ann then testified about how Miranda drove her back to her neighborhood and how she went home and told her sister what had happened.

After a fifteen-minute recess, Alvin Moore had his opportunity to ask Lois Ann questions. When a witness testifies for one side in

A defense attorney cross-examines a witness (left) during a trial in an attempt to cast doubt on the witness's testimony.

a trial, the attorney for the other side can also ask him or her questions. This questioning of a witness by the attorney for the other side is called cross-examination and can often bring out inconsistencies in the witness's testimony. During cross-examination, an attorney will try to convince the jury that the witness's testimony is inaccurate in some regard.

Moore's questions focused on Lois Ann's statements that she did not physically struggle because Miranda was stronger than she was and had threatened her. He tried to plant a seed of doubt in the jury's mind with his last questions:

Q. You are a young girl, do you know the difference between rape and seduction?

A. Yes.

Q. If you know the difference, did the defendant rape you, or did he seduce you?

A. He raped me.

MR. MOORE: No further questions.

MR. TUROFF: I have no further questions.

THE COURT: That is all, Ma'am, you may step down.[18]

That was the end of Lois Ann's testimony.

The next witness was Lois Ann's sister Sarah. Her testimony was very short. Turoff asked her to describe Lois Ann's appearance when she came home that night. Sarah stated that "she came home, pounded on the door, her hair was all over like she had been in a fight, and her dress was brand new, a new suit, and it was a mess, and she was crying and carrying on, and I asked her what was the matter, and she would not tell me."[19] When Lois Ann told her what had happened, Sarah testified, she called the police. Alvin Moore did not cross-examine Sarah.

Detective Cooley's Testimony

The third witness of the morning was Detective Carroll Cooley. Turoff asked him questions about Miranda's confession. Detective Cooley described the interrogation session very generally and without detail about what happened:

Q. Who was present during this discussion, Officer?

A. Myself, Detective Young and the defendant.

Q. Do you know approximately what time of day this took place?

A. Approximately 11:30.

Q. Was that on March 13th?

A. Yes, Sir.

Q. 11:30, is that a.m. or p.m.?

A. A.M.

Q. Now, during the period, let's say the period of time you had first arrested or picked up the defendant, brought him to the police department and then had the interrogation with him, was he in your custody all during that period of time?

A. Yes, Sir, he was.

Q. During that period of time, did you make any threats or use any force on the defendant?

A. No, Sir.

Q. During this period of time, did you make the defendant any promises of immunity if he would have this discussion with you?

A. No, Sir, I did not.

Q. Did any other officers in your presence do any of these acts?

A. No, Sir.[20]

Detective Cooley then described how Miranda had first denied raping Lois Ann and how, "after a short time," he changed his story and admitted that he had used force against her and had sexual intercourse with her. The detective testified that after he confessed, Miranda wrote his statement down. Turoff asked the judge to accept the written confession into evidence, a ruling that would allow the jury to read it.

Before receiving the written confession into evidence, Moore was allowed to ask Detective Cooley about the interrogation. Such questions about how a document like a confession was obtained are called voir dire. Moore concentrated on questions about whether the detectives told Miranda before he confessed that he was entitled to consult with an attorney:

Q. Officer Cooley, in the taking of this statement, what did you say to the defendant to get him to make this statement?

A. I asked the defendant if he would tell us, write the same story that he had just told me, and he said that he would.

Q. Did you warn him of his rights?

A. Yes, Sir, at the heading of the statement is a paragraph typed out, and I read this paragraph to him out loud.

Q. Did you read that to him out loud?

A. Yes, Sir.

Q. But did you ever, before or during your conversation or before taking this statement, did you ever advise the defendant he was entitled to the services of an attorney?

A. When I read—

Q. Before he made any statement?

A. When I read the statement right there.

Q. I don't see in the statement that it says where he is entitled to the advice of an attorney before he made it.

A. No, Sir.

Q. It is not in that statement?

A. It doesn't say anything about an attorney. Would you like for me to read it?

Q. No, it will be an exhibit if it is admitted and the jury can read it, but you didn't tell him he could have an attorney?

MR. TUROFF: This is not proper voir dire. He may go into this on cross-examination, but this is not proper voir dire.

THE COURT: Sustained.

MR. MOORE: We object because the Supreme Court of the United States says a man is entitled to an attorney at the time of arrest.

MR. TUROFF: State offers in evidence State's Exhibit 1 [the confession] for identification.

THE COURT: Objection is overruled, may be admitted, Exhibit 1 in evidence.[21]

Moore thus objected to the jury's seeing the written confession on the ground that Miranda had not been given the opportunity to consult with a lawyer at the start of the interrogation. Judge McFate denied the objection, applying the then-established rule that all voluntary confessions are admissible as evidence, regardless of whether the accused had legal counsel. The confession was received into evidence.

After a lunch break, the prosecution presented its final witness, Detective Wilfred Young, who had also been present at Miranda's verbal confession. Detective Young testified that neither he nor his partner threatened Miranda. He also testified that they did not use any force on him or make him any promises of immunity. In response to Moore's only two questions on cross-examination, Detective Young stated that no attorney was present at the interrogation and that neither he nor his partner had told Miranda that he had a right to have an attorney with him during interrogation.

On behalf of the prosecution, Turoff completed his case after presenting the testimony of the four witnesses and the written confession. Moore presented no witnesses or other evidence. Miranda did not testify, primarily because of the legal rule that the past criminal record of a criminal defendant can be given to the jury only when the defendant testifies at trial. Miranda did not want the jury to learn of his past criminal convictions. Moore would simply try during his closing summation to convince the jury that the prosecutor's evidence did not prove beyond a reasonable doubt that Miranda kidnapped and raped Lois Ann Jameson.

The Lawyers' Summations

In a trial, once all the evidence has been presented to a jury, the attorneys for each side have the opportunity to talk to the jury to convince it that the evidence favors their client. These arguments to the jury are known as summations. In criminal trials in Arizona in 1963, the prosecutor argued first, the defense attorney argued next, and then the prosecutor had a final chance to convince the jury. These summations are not themselves evidence;

they are supposed to summarize for the jury the evidence that has already been presented.

Lawrence Turoff began his argument by reminding the jury about the events that Lois Ann described. He summarized her testimony about that night, beginning with her leaving work, through Miranda's forcing her into the car and raping her, and ending with her conversation with her sister at home. Turoff then spoke to the jury about the written confession. He held the confession in his hand and discussed how Miranda had forced Lois Ann into his car. Turoff suggested to the jury that Miranda was wrong in saying that he didn't use any force against Lois Ann:

> You have this [the written confession] to take with you to the deliberation room. This is his written statement. You have read it all. He admits stopping the girl walking up

THE ROLE OF THE JURY IN CRIMINAL TRIALS

In criminal trials, the jury's job is to listen to all the testimony and decide which witnesses to believe. The jury must weigh the evidence that is presented during the trial and reach a decision on whether the defendant is guilty or innocent.

The jury should base its decision only on the evidence it heard at trial. It cannot rely on newspaper or television reports of the crime or of the trial. In some trials, the judge will sequester the jury, which means that its members do not go home during the trial. This is done to make certain that only admissible evidence is considered. For example, if newspapers were to report that a confession exists, that could affect the jury's verdict even if the judge ruled that the document could not be used in the trial.

Before a trial can begin, jurors must swear that they will use integrity when analyzing the evidence presented and render a verdict accordingly.

the street. He admits seeing a little ahead of her and getting out of the car. He admits grabbing her by the arm.

Here's where the story starts to change. He said he asked
her to get into the car. He said she got into the car without force. Here we go back together again—he says he
tied her hands and ankles. If you believe she willingly
got in the car with him, what was the need of tying her
up? Why did he tie her up if she readily went along with
what he wanted to do?[22]

Turoff then compared Miranda's confession (in which he said
that Lois Ann cooperated with him in getting undressed) with
Lois Ann's testimony (in which she said that Miranda used force
and threats against her).

Turoff concluded his summation with the following statement:

The only issue you have in front of you is whether or not
the act of sexual intercourse was because her resistance
was overcome by force or violence. We submit that all
the evidence you have heard just recently would indicate that the latter is the correct interpretation, that she
did not willfully get in that car. The inconsistencies between what the defendant said took place and what she
tells us today are inconsistencies that are in her favor. If
she did willfully do what he would have you believe she
did, there would have been no need for him to tie her
up. We submit to you that her acts after she had been
dropped off by the defendant, is consistent with the fact
she did not go with him willfully. She did not enter into
this act of intercourse with him willfully, but in fact, she
was forced to, by his own force and violence, directed
against her.[23]

Turoff then thanked the jury for its attention and sat down.

Alvin Moore then arose and addressed the jury on behalf of
Ernesto Miranda. He began by saying that rape cases are un-
comfortable for lawyers and jurors but that they all had a civic

THE ART OF THE SUMMATION

After all the evidence has been heard, the lawyers for both parties get to talk to the jury before it begins its deliberations. This is an opportunity to weave all the evidence together in a story that will win either an acquittal (in the case of the defense) or a conviction (in the case of the prosecution). Indeed, a common saying among lawyers is that when a client comes to the office for the first time with his or her tale of legal woe, the lawyer should already start thinking about how best to argue the case to a jury in final summation.

A New York district attorney passionately presents his summation while the opposing counsel busily takes notes.

Some lawyers approach summation in a coolly logical fashion. They talk about the key items of evidence and put them in the best light possible for their client. A prosecutor, for instance, will emphasize the evidence that points to the defendant's guilt while telling the jury why it should not believe evidence that points to innocence. The attorney for the defendant will argue in an opposite manner, putting the most emphasis on evidence that might raise in the jurors' minds a reasonable doubt about the defendant's guilt.

Some lawyers employ great eloquence and displays of emotion in summation. The most eloquent lawyers often attract a large crowd to their summations. Those crowds include many other lawyers, who both enjoy the drama and hope to learn some tips on summation from the masters.

---

duty to play these roles. The heart of his argument was that Lois Ann's lack of physical resistance created a reasonable doubt about whether she had sexual intercourse voluntarily or by force:

> Now, let's get down to this crime of rape and see what happens. The Court will instruct you as to the amount of resistance required on the part of the prosecuting witness before she is forced to the act of sexual intercourse.

There is no going into the background of Lois Ann Jameson to see whether she's a good girl or a bad girl. We must assume and you must assume she was a good girl and virtuous up until that time.

But you assume that, you've also got to assume she's going to resist the attentions of this male, the attentions of the defendant. What resistance was shown here? Where did she resist?

Under the law, he could have carried her for two hours and 40 minutes around in the car, all this time, and if a split second before the sexual intercourse occurred, she consented, he didn't forcibly and by force and violence have sexual intercourse with her.

The only evidence of force and violence that you have at all in this case is where he grabbed her by the arm, put her in the car and grabbed a piece of rope out of thin air somewhere and tied her ankles and her hands. That is the only force and violence that was ever used. The disrobing act or disrobing deal, he could have held her arms close to her. How could he have disrobed her? Did she resist? No, she didn't resist him taking her clothes off. She never resisted at all except her testimony she kind of pushed him away while he was on top of her, but he was stronger than she was. Now, that is not the kind of resistance that is required of a prosecuting witness in a case of rape. The kind of resistance that is required is that she resists and resists until she can resist no longer. There is no evidence of that fact here. That just did not happen.[24]

After Moore finished his argument, Turoff gave a brief final argument and quickly sat down.

The Judge's Instructions to the Jury

The next step in the trial was for Judge McFate to tell the jury about the law that they had to apply in deciding whether Miranda

The Role of the Judge in Criminal Trials Before a Jury

In most criminal trials, the jury has the role of evaluating the evidence and deciding the factual issues that determine guilt or innocence. The judge has the equally important job of applying the law to the operation of the trial. One part of that job is applying the rules of evidence to decide whether the jury should see a particular item of evidence. For instance, a jury is not supposed to hear about a confession that was forced out of a defendant by violence. If a defendant claims that his or her confession is invalid for such a reason, the judge will hear evidence about the confession with the jury not present, usually before the trial even begins. If the judge decides that the confession is valid, the prosecution is free to bring it up during the trial. If the judge decides that the confession is invalid, the prosecution cannot introduce it at trial, and the jury will never even hear of its existence. The judge administers many other rules of evidence in deciding which evidence will be allowed to go before the jury. Although the jury decides guilt or innocence based on the evidence it hears, the judge can decide what evidence the jury will hear.

The judge also has the important role of telling the jury what the law is regarding the crimes of which the defendant is accused. The judge informs the jury what facts must be proven in order to find the defendant guilty. The jury decides whether the defendant is guilty or innocent, but the judge tells the jury which facts are relevant to that decision.

was guilty of kidnapping and rape. As to Lois Ann's resistance, Judge McFate gave a one-sentence summary of the law: "In order to constitute the crime of rape in the first degree by overcoming resistance by force and violence, it must appear that the victim has resisted to the utmost." The judge gave the jury a much longer instruction on the issue of Miranda's confession:

> If, under my instructions, you find that a voluntary confession was made, you are the exclusive judges as to whether or not the confession was true. The fact that the Court has admitted into evidence the alleged confession of this defendant does not bind the jury to accept the Court's conclusion, and the jury, before it may take a confession into consideration, must for itself find whether or not it was a voluntary confession. . . .

A confession is involuntary when it is obtained by any sort of violence or threats, or by any direct or implied promises of immunity or benefit, or by any improper influence which might induce in the mind of the defendant, the belief or hope that he would gain or benefit or be better off by making a statement, and when the defendant makes such confession as a result of any such inducement originating with a law enforcement officer. But the fact that a defendant was under arrest at the time he made a confession or that he was not at the time represented by counsel or that he was not told that any statement he might make could or would be used against him, in and of themselves, will not render such confession involuntary.[25]

This statement of the law regarding confession would be closely examined when the case was later reviewed on appeal to higher courts.

The Verdict

At 3:37 in the afternoon, the jury went into the jury room to decide the case. With no one else present, the twelve jurors discussed the evidence. That evening, they returned to the courtroom and told Judge McFate that they found Ernesto Miranda guilty beyond a reasonable doubt of kidnapping and rape.

The *Arizona Republic* reported the trial in its edition of June 21, 1963. Under a headline of "Jury Convicts Phoenician," the paper stated:

A Superior Court jury last night found Ernest Arthur Miranda, 23, of 2525 W. Mariposa, guilty of kidnapping and raping an 18-year-old girl March 3.

Judge Yale McFate set sentencing for 1:30 p.m. Thursday.

The jury of nine men and three women deliberated more than five hours before they returned the verdict.

The girl testified that Miranda forced her into his car as she walked home alone at midnight near a northeast bus stop, tied her hands and feet with a rope and threatened her with a sharp instrument.

She said Miranda then drove her into the desert east of town and raped her. After returning to Phoenix, the girl told the jury, Miranda asked her to pray for him.

In another jury trial before Judge McFate on Wednesday, Miranda was convicted of the $8 robbery last November of a 23-year-old woman.[26]

One week later, on June 27, 1963, Judge McFate imposed a prison sentence of between twenty and thirty years on the two charges of kidnapping and rape. On the charge of robbery for which he had been tried separately, Miranda received another sentence of between twenty and twenty-five years. It seemed as if Ernesto Miranda would be behind bars for most of the rest of his life.

Chapter 4

The Appeal to the Arizona Supreme Court

AFTER JUDGE MCFATE IMPOSED his sentence, the prison authorities transferred Ernesto Miranda to the Arizona State Prison in the town of Florence. Located in a remote desert area, the prison consisted of several ugly buildings surrounded by a high wall that separated the prison world from the free world. In this grim setting, Miranda settled into his new life. The prison staff trained him to be a barber, and he spent his days giving haircuts to the other convicts.

Outside the prison walls, Miranda's lawyer was still trying to get him freed. In all criminal trials, a defendant who is convicted of a crime can ask a higher court to examine his or her case to see whether he or she was unfairly convicted. Taking a case to a higher court is called an appeal. The higher courts that hear appeals are called appellate courts. Each of the fifty states has one or more appellate courts. In Arizona, the only state appellate court (in 1963) was the Arizona Supreme Court. It was to that court that Miranda's lawyer, Alvin Moore, appealed his convictions.

How Criminal Appeals Work

Most criminal appeals consist of two steps. In the first step, the attorney for the convicted defendant writes a legal paper called a brief. In that paper, which is usually between twenty and fifty pages, the attorney writes down all the reasons why his or her client's conviction was unfair. The attorney directs the judges to

FEDERAL BUREAU OF INVESTIGATION, UNITED STATES DEPARTMENT OF JUSTICE		
WASHINGTON, D.C.		
CURRENT ARREST OR RECEIPT		
DATE ARRESTED OR RECEIVED	CHARGE OR OFFENSE (If code citation is used it should be accompanied by charge)	DISPOSITION OR SENTENCE (List FINAL disposition only. If not now available, submit later on FBI Form R-84 for completion of record.)
-5-1963 MARICOPA COUNTY	COUNT I-KIDNAPPING COUNT II-RAPE(FIRST DEGREE) TO RUN CONCURRENTLY	20 yrs. to 30 yrs.
OCCUPATION TRUCK DRIVER	RESIDENCE OF PERSON FINGERPRINTED WIFE: TWILA MIRANDA 157 E. COMMONWELL CHANDLER, ARIZONA	

If COLLECT wire reply or COLLECT telephone reply is desired, indicate here

☐ Wire reply   ☐ Telephone reply

Telephone number

FOR INSTITUTIONS USE ONLY

Sentence expires... 7-5-1993

INSTRUCTIONS

1. FORWARD ARREST CARDS TO FBI IMMEDIATELY AFTER FINGERPRINTING FOR MOST EFFECTIVE SERVICE.
2. TYPE or PRINT all information.
3. Note imputations in proper finger squares.
4. REPLY WILL QUOTE ONLY NUMBER APPEARING IN THE BLOCK MARKED "CONTRIBUTOR'S NO."
5. Indicate any additional copies for other agencies in space below—include their complete mailing address.

SEND COPY TO:

Jos M. Rodriguez, Secretary
ARIZONA STATE PRISON

The Federal Bureau of Investigation's arrest card for Ernesto Miranda lists his convictions and sentence as well as his somber mug shot.

pages of the trial transcript that (he or she argues) show that the trial judge made a legal mistake. For example, if the judge let the jury hear evidence that it should not have heard or the judge described the law incorrectly to the jury, those would be considered legal errors. The attorney argues in the brief that his or her client was illegally convicted and should either be freed or given a new trial. The lawyer delivers copies of the brief to the appellate court and to the prosecution.

The prosecution then will submit its own written brief to the appellate court and deliver a copy to the defendant's attorney. In that brief, the prosecution usually argues that the defendant's claims are wrong and that the conviction resulted from a proper and fair trial. Each of the judges of the appellate court then reads the briefs from both sides and looks at the parts of the trial transcript that are at issue in the appeal.

In stage two of an appeal, the lawyers come to the appellate court on a scheduled day and present their arguments in person to the judges. This is called the oral argument of the appeal. Oral argument of an appeal is very different from the trial of the same case. Whereas during a trial witnesses are questioned by lawyers, at the appellate court the witnesses do not come to testify again. The appellate court considers only the testimony that was already given at the trial and recorded word for word on paper by the courtroom stenographer. Appellate courts almost always have three or more judges hearing the arguments in each case. In the Arizona Supreme Court, five judges (officially called justices) sat on the bench in front of a special courtroom in Phoenix.

At oral argument, the lawyer for the convicted defendant addresses the court first. He or she argues that, for the reasons written in the brief, his or her client's conviction should be reversed. The judges ask that lawyer questions about his or her arguments. After the lawyer for the defendant finishes speaking, the lawyer for the prosecution addresses the court. That lawyer tries to persuade the judges that the trial reached the right result. The appellate judges typically do not announce a result on the spot. They decide the case in private conferences after they have heard the oral argument of both sides. Usually, they write an explanation of the reasoning behind their decision and send that decision to the parties in one or two months. They may affirm the conviction, which means that it stays in effect, or reverse the conviction, which means that either a new trial must be held or the criminal charges will be dropped altogether.

The Briefs to the Arizona Supreme Court

In his briefs (dated December 10, 1963), Alvin Moore pointed to six possible errors in Miranda's trials, five of which would be rejected by the Arizona Supreme Court and be quickly forgotten. The sixth error that Moore claimed, however, would eventually make newspaper headlines. Moore argued that Judge McFate had made a serious mistake at the trials by allowing the juries to hear about the interrogation and to see Miranda's written confession. Moore argued that the juries were convinced of Miranda's guilt mostly because of the confession that they never should have heard about. He argued that the convictions were thus illegal and that Miranda should be given a new trial.

Alvin Moore based his briefs on the highest law of the country, the U.S. Constitution. In addition to setting out the basic framework for the federal government, the Constitution also guarantees certain basic rights (such as freedom of speech and trial by jury) to individuals throughout the country, regardless of the laws of the fifty states. The Constitution went into effect in 1788 and has been amended (that is, parts changed or new parts added) almost thirty times since then.

Moore relied specifically on the part of the Fourteenth Amendment to the Constitution that states, "No State shall . . . deprive any person of life, liberty, or property, without due process of law." The phrase "due process of law" has a long history and has been interpreted many ways by judges and lawyers. Perhaps the simplest interpretation is that "due process" requires that nobody

Since it went into effect in 1788, the Constitution has served as the supreme law of the United States, protecting the rights of American citizens.

THE SELECTIVE INCORPORATION DOCTRINE

The U.S. Constitution went into effect in 1788, creating the three-branch federal government that still exists today. Congress and the states added the first ten amendments to the Constitution in 1791. These ten amendments are known as the Bill of Rights, for they forbid the federal government from infringing on certain rights of individual Americans. The many rights protected by the Bill of Rights include freedom of speech and freedom of religion (First Amendment), freedom from unreasonable searches (Fourth Amendment), and the right to trial by jury (Sixth and Seventh Amendments).

The Bill of Rights, however, was adopted to restrain the power of the federal government. It did not apply to the state governments. Indeed, in the early nineteenth century, some states did some things that would now be considered unconstitutional, such as supporting an established church.

The Bill of Rights, which comprises the first ten amendments to the U.S. Constitution, was adopted in 1791.

After the Civil War, Congress approved and the states ratified the Fourteenth Amendment to the Constitution, which requires the states to comply with due process of law when depriving any person of life, liberty, or property. Most lawyers and judges believed that the due process clause merely required the states to act with fundamental fairness toward the persons who come within the reach of their laws. Some lawyers and judges, however, believed that the due process clause made the Bill of Rights binding on the states as well as on the federal government.

Over time, the Supreme Court has decided many cases in which it has applied various parts of the Bill of Rights in deciding whether to uphold convictions in state courts. The theory that parts of the Bill of Rights apply to the states is known as the selective incorporation doctrine. Although the Court used the Fourteenth Amendment to enforce the Bill of Rights during the first half of the twentieth Century, it began doing so regularly only in the 1960s, beginning with the landmark 1961 case of *Mapp v. Ohio*. Almost all of the criminal law guarantees of the Bill of Rights have now been applied to the states through the Fourteenth Amendment.

can be deprived of his or her life, liberty, or property without a fair trial that follows fair procedures.

Moore argued in his brief that Miranda's trial was unfair (that is, a denial of due process) because Judge McFate allowed the jury to hear about the confession even though the police had interrogated Miranda without first appointing a lawyer to advise him. It was only fair, Moore argued, to let Miranda consult first with a lawyer, who would have told him of his right to remain silent and probably would have advised him not to confess to any crime.

Moore argued that a recent decision of the U.S. Supreme Court supported his argument on behalf of Miranda. In *Gideon v. Wainwright*, a 1963 decision, the Supreme Court ruled that, under the Fourteenth Amendment, any criminal defendant charged with serious criminal charges is entitled to have a court-appointed lawyer represent him or her at trial if the defendant cannot afford to hire an attorney. In that case, the Supreme

A defendant consults with his attorneys while in court. In addition to ensuring a fair trial, such legal representation can also help defendants better understand their constitutional rights.

EARLIER CASES ON POLICE INTERROGATION

In the 1930s and 1940s, the Supreme Court began to reverse criminal convictions in state courts. When examining state prosecutions, the Court asked whether the treatment of the defendant was fundamentally fair—that is, whether the behavior of the state complied with due process of law, a general standard under which most police interrogations would be approved. Some cases, however, were so disturbing that they failed the due process test.

In the 1936 case of *Brown v. Mississippi*, the Supreme Court reviewed the murder convictions of three men who had been tried in the state courts of Mississippi. The three illiterate black defendants were whipped and beaten until they confessed to murder. The state argued to the Supreme Court that the confessions were valid evidence because the Fifth Amendment right to remain silent did not apply in state criminal proceedings. The Supreme Court reversed the convictions. Chief Justice Charles Evans Hughes wrote the decision for the Court, stating that regardless of the Fifth Amendment's restriction to federal proceedings, the police behavior had violated the due process clause of the Fourteenth Amendment. Chief Justice Hughes stated that "it would be difficult to conceive of methods more revolting to the sense of justice than those taken to procure the confessions of these petitioners, and the use of the confessions thus obtained as the basis for conviction and sentence was a clear denial of due process."

Physical beatings were not the only method used to force confessions out of suspects. In the 1940 case of *Chambers v. Florida*, the Supreme Court reversed the convictions of four men who were interrogated for long periods over five days, with little food or opportunity for sleep allowed to them. In the 1944 case of *Ashcraft v. Tennessee*, the Court reversed the conviction of a man who confessed after thirty-six hours of nonstop interrogation. Such abusive treatment of suspects, the Court ruled, violated the due process clause.

Court held that the right to due process in state-court trials under the Fourteenth Amendment includes the same right to counsel that the Sixth Amendment guarantees in federal-court trials. Although *Gideon v. Wainwright* was about the appointment of an attorney at the time of trial, Moore argued that the same right is in effect when a criminal suspect is taken into custody and interrogated about a crime.

The prosecution then submitted its own brief to the Arizona Supreme Court. The Arizona attorney general, Darrel F. Smith, represented the state and argued that the convictions did not violate due process because Miranda had no right to an appointed attorney at the time of interrogation. With many other cases also awaiting hearings, the Arizona Supreme Court did not bother with the usual second step of the appellate process. The court told Moore and the attorney general that there would be no oral argument of this case before the five justices of the court. They would decide the case based on only the written briefs submitted by both sides.

The Decision of the Arizona Supreme Court

On April 22, 1965, the Arizona Supreme Court issued its written decisions in Ernesto Miranda's two cases, the kidnapping and rape of Lois Ann Jameson and the separate robbery case. Justice Ernest W. McFarland wrote the decisions, with which the other four justices all agreed. The supreme court affirmed (upheld) all of Miranda's convictions. The court rejected Alvin Moore's arguments about the legality of the confession. Judge McFarland emphasized the fact that Miranda had confessed without any force or threats by the police. Because the confession was voluntary, Arizona law required Judge McFate to let the jury hear about it.

As to the constitutional argument raised by Moore, Justice McFarland held that the police had not violated Miranda's due process rights by interrogating him without the advice of a lawyer because Miranda had not asked to consult an attorney at the time of his interrogation. At one point of his written decision, Justice McFarland discussed the tension between individual rights and the interests of law enforcement:

> What is the purpose of the right to counsel? What is the purpose of the Sixth and Fourteenth Amendments? Without question it is to protect individual rights that we cherish, but there must be a balance between the competing interests of society and the rights of the individual. Society has the right of protection against those who roam the streets for the purpose of violating the law, but that protection must not be at the expense of the rights of the individual guaranteed under the Sixth and Fourteenth Amendments to our Constitution.[27]

Seeking Review by the U.S. Supreme Court

By the time the Arizona Supreme Court rejected his appeal, Ernesto Miranda had already been in prison for two years. It appeared that he would be a prison barber for many years to come. For most people convicted of a crime in a state court, an appeal to the state supreme court is the end of the judicial line. If, however, the convicted defendant claims a violation of a right guaranteed to him or her by the Constitution, the defendant can ask the U.S. Supreme Court to hear his or her appeal. Located in Washington, D.C., the Supreme Court is the highest federal court of the nation. The Court consists of nine judges (known as justices), all appointed by the president and approved by the Senate for lifetime terms. The Supreme Court is the final interpreter of federal laws,

HOW CASES GET TO THE SUPREME COURT

Many people who lose a court case proclaim that they will take their case all the way to the U.S. Supreme Court. Very few of these people actually succeed in having the Supreme Court consider the merits of their case. One explanation for this fact is that the Supreme Court has a special and narrow mission. It does not primarily exist to correct injustices that may have occurred in individual cases. The lower federal appellate courts (known as the U.S. courts of appeals) and the numerous state appellate courts have the mission of addressing most legal errors and injustices. The chief mission of the Supreme Court is to resolve unclear questions of federal law. The Court looks for cases that will enable it to make a decision that will guide all other courts on a specific issue of federal law in the future.

To help the Court fulfill that mission, Congress has passed laws that allow the Court to pick the cases it wishes to hear from among those whose parties ask for review. Since 1925, the Supreme Court has had the discretion to accept or deny most cases for review. Those cases can come from the U.S. courts of appeals and from the state appellate courts. If a case does not involve an issue of federal law, the Supreme Court cannot review it.

The Supreme Court accepts only about 5 percent of the cases that parties urge it to take. One reason the Court might agree to hear a case is that the lower federal appellate courts and the state appellate courts have reached different conclusions on how federal law applies in the case. Only about one hundred cases satisfy this standard and are reviewed by the Supreme Court in a typical year.

including the Constitution. The Court has the authority to hear appeals of state appellate-court decisions that involve rights guaranteed by the U.S. Constitution. With only a few technical exceptions, the Supreme Court can choose whether or not it wishes to hear a case; usually, it accepts only cases in which an important issue of law is involved.

Alvin Moore's appointment to represent Miranda expired once the Arizona Supreme Court issued its decision, and as he did not want to represent him any longer, Miranda was on his own. Miranda himself wrote a document, called a petition for a writ of certiorari, asking the U.S. Supreme Court to hear his case. The clerk's office of the Court sent his petition back to him, indicating that he had not included a copy of the final judgment of the Arizona Supreme Court, as required by the U.S. Supreme Court rules.

Miranda then received one of the few breaks he'd ever had in his life. The head of the Phoenix office of the American Civil Liberties Union (ACLU), Robert Corcoran, read the Arizona Supreme Court decision in Miranda's case and took interest. The ACLU is an organization that pursues cases that involve the legal rights of individuals. Corcoran thought that the U.S. Supreme Court should decide whether a poor person is entitled to legal representation during interrogation by the police. Corcoran convinced two lawyers in the Phoenix law firm of Lewis, Roca, Scoville, Beauchamps, and Linton to represent Miranda pro bono (that is, free of charge): John J. Flynn, a prominent criminal trial lawyer, and John P. Frank, an experienced appellate lawyer.

Flynn and Frank, with the help of other attorneys in their law firm, wrote a new petition for a writ of certiorari in July 1965. In their petition, they asked the Supreme Court to take Miranda's case and resolve the unsettled issue of whether an attorney must be appointed for a poor person who is under police interrogation for a crime. In August 1965, an assistant attorney general for the State of Arizona, Gary K. Nelson, sent a short legal document to the Supreme Court indicating that the Arizona attorney general agreed that the U.S. Supreme Court should resolve the unsettled legal issue of whether attorneys must be appointed for poor suspects at interrogations.

John J. Flynn (left), a distinguished criminal trial attorney, represented Miranda (right) during his Supreme Court appeal along with cocounsel John P. Frank.

On November 22, 1965, the U.S. Supreme Court responded by agreeing to hear four cases involving police interrogations. One of these was Miranda's case. The nine justices of the Court had met in conference and agreed to use these four cases to clarify the law about interrogations. Ernesto Miranda's case was going to the highest court in the nation.

Chapter 5

At the U.S. Supreme Court

Back in the Arizona State Prison in Florence, Ernesto Miranda was delighted that his case was going to the Supreme Court. He had another chance to get out of the long prison term he was serving. He wrote letters to his new lawyers, thanking them for their help.

John Flynn and Gary Nelson were also happy that Miranda's case was going to Washington. Arguing an appeal at the U.S. Supreme Court is a great honor for a lawyer, and few lawyers ever get the chance to do so. Flynn would argue the case for Miranda, while Nelson would argue for the prosecution. For both of them, this was their first U.S. Supreme Court argument.

Many other lawyers, politicians, and members of the public also became interested in Miranda's case and in the other three cases that the Court would be hearing regarding confessions in criminal cases. "Law and order" was becoming an important legal and political issue in the United States in the mid-1960s. Under the leadership of Chief Justice Earl Warren, the Supreme Court had decided, usually under the due process clause of the Fourteenth Amendment to the U.S. Constitution, that state courts must adopt certain procedural safeguards to protect the rights of defendants. Some people approved of these Supreme Court decisions, believing that Supreme Court intervention was the only way to stop unfair practices by local police and state courts. Other people, like Barry Goldwater, the Republican nominee for president in 1964, disapproved of these decisions, believing that the Supreme Court was hindering legitimate police efforts to fight crime and protect the public. In an atmosphere charged with fear of crime and with political ambitions, the local Arizona criminal case would become famous across the nation.

The Brief for Miranda

In their brief, Miranda's attorneys did not argue that he was innocent of the crime charged. They instead argued that he was entitled to a new trial because the jury should never have been allowed to hear his confession. Frank and Flynn argued that a poor criminal suspect who is being interrogated while in the custody of local police must be offered the services of an appointed attorney before he or she answers any questions. They argued that because the Phoenix police did not arrange for a lawyer to advise Miranda, his confession should not have been allowed into evidence at his trials. In the brief, the two lawyers stated that the "question presented" by Miranda's appeal was "whether the confession of a poorly educated, mentally abnormal, indigent [impoverished] defendant, not told of his right to counsel, taken while he is in police custody and without the assistance of counsel, which was not requested, can be admitted into evidence over specific objection based on the absence of counsel."[28] Frank and Flynn based their argument on the due process clause of the Fourteenth Amendment and on the Sixth Amendment, which guarantees to criminal defendants in federal courts the right "to have the Assistance of Counsel for his defense." The Sixth Amendment was relevant to Miranda's appeal because recent Supreme Court decisions had held that the "due process" guaranteed to state defendants by the Fourteenth Amendment included the same right to counsel guaranteed to federal defendants by the Sixth Amendment.

Miranda's lawyers conceded that no Supreme Court decision had yet held that a state criminal defendant is entitled to the appointment of a lawyer at the time of interrogation if he or she cannot afford to hire one. They argued, however, that recent

Supreme Court decisions supported such an extension of constitutional law. They noted that in *Gideon v. Wainwright*, a 1963
case, the Supreme Court had held that state courts must appoint
attorneys to represent poor criminal defendants on trial for serious charges.

Frank and Flynn also cited another case, *Escobedo v. Illinois*,
in which the Supreme Court had held in 1964 that local police
who are interrogating a criminal suspect in custody must allow
the suspect to consult with his or her private attorney when the
suspect asks to do so. The question presented by Miranda's case
was whether the state must appoint an attorney to advise a criminal suspect during interrogation, regardless of whether the suspect asks to speak to an attorney.

Miranda's lawyers further argued that the police must tell
the indigent suspect in interrogation of this right to an appointed
attorney. In the brief, Miranda's lawyers stated that "it is, after
all, the man's privilege to be silent" and that "it does smack of
denial of equal protection to say that this is a right only for those
well educated enough to know about it." [29]

Miranda's lawyers conceded that state governments would
have to spend money on providing attorneys to criminal suspects
in interrogation. They also conceded that opinions differed on
whether providing attorneys to criminal suspects in interrogation
would make law enforcement significantly harder. They argued
that whatever costs and burdens the new ruling might cause,
they were worth it to protect the rights of poor people who were
suspected of crimes but did not know of their rights during interrogation.

The Other Briefs

Gary Nelson answered Miranda's brief by submitting one on behalf of the State of Arizona. In his brief, Nelson emphasized the
facts that the police had not threatened or abused Miranda and
that the police had advised him of his right to remain silent. Nelson argued that Miranda had voluntarily confessed to his crimes.

Nelson went on to explain that the *Escobedo* case was factu-
ally different from Miranda's case. In *Escobedo*, the suspect had

ESCOBEDO V. ILLINOIS

One of the key precedents upon which Miranda's lawyers relied was the 1964 Supreme Court decision in *Escobedo v. Illinois*. That case involved a twenty-two-year-old Mexican American laborer named Danny Escobedo. In 1960, the police arrested him and an accomplice for the murder of Escobedo's brother-in-law. The police interrogated the two men separately. While being interrogated, Escobedo asked several times that his lawyer be present with him.

He had previously retained a lawyer in connection with a personal injury case. The police lied to him and told him that his lawyer did not want to see him. The lawyer found out about the arrest and came to the police station, but the police would not let him consult with Escobedo. By accident, Escobedo and his lawyer saw each other for a few seconds through an open door. They waved at each other, but the police quickly closed the door. After hours of interrogation, Escobedo confessed to the crime. He was convicted of murder and sentenced to twenty years in prison. The Illinois Supreme Court affirmed his conviction.

Danny Escobedo, the defendant in the 1964 benchmark case of Escobedo v. Illinois.

The U.S. Supreme Court reversed the conviction. Justice Arthur Goldberg wrote the Court's opinion, joined by Chief Justice Warren and Justices Black, Douglas, and Brennan. The Court held that the right to the advice of counsel extends not just to criminal defendants at trial but also to criminal suspects whom the police are interrogating. One factor distinguishing *Escobedo* from *Miranda* was that Danny Escobedo asked to see his retained attorney, whereas Ernesto Miranda did not ask to see an attorney and could not afford to hire one.

previously hired a lawyer and had asked to consult with him when the police began their interrogation. The police, however, falsely told Escobedo that the lawyer did not want to talk with him. In contrast, Miranda had not asked to consult with a lawyer, and the police had not lied to him.

Nelson further argued that the Supreme Court should not expand its interpretation of the Fourteenth Amendment as Miranda was requesting. Finally, he asserted that the Supreme Court should not hinder police efforts to obtain confessions, at least in cases where no threats or force is used, because society needs to protect itself by obtaining confessions from criminals who are willing to make them.

In important cases, organizations not directly involved in the case will sometimes submit briefs to the appellate court stating their opinions on a particular legal issue. A person or organization submitting such a brief is called an amicus curiae (Latin for "friend of the court"). The briefs are known as amicus briefs. In Miranda's case and the three companion cases involving interrogation, three amicus briefs were submitted. One brief was written on behalf of the attorneys general (the top government lawyers) of twenty-nine states. Another brief was written by lawyers of the National District Attorneys Association, an organization representing prosecutors throughout the country. Both of these briefs stated that police interrogation was an important tool in fighting crime and that the Supreme Court should allow police to interrogate poor suspects without the presence of an attorney as long as no force or threats were used.

The American Civil Liberties Union submitted the third amicus brief, asking the Supreme Court to require the appointment of an attorney for any poor suspect being interrogated while in police custody. The ACLU brief was important because it used different legal reasoning than Miranda's lawyers did. Miranda's attorneys argued that his right to a lawyer, located in the Sixth Amendment to the Constitution and incorporated into the due process guarantee of the Fourteenth Amendment, required the appointment of counsel at the time of interrogation. The ACLU focused instead on a suspect's right not to incriminate himself or herself (that is, not to confess). That right is located in the Fifth Amendment (covering federal prosecutions) and is also a part of the due process guarantee of the Fourteenth Amendment (which covers state prosecutions). According to the ACLU, "police custodial interrogation designed to elicit a confession is inherently compelling—inherently violative of the privilege against self-incrimination." In other words, just being held by the police is so threatening that suspects may feel forced to confess. This is because the suspect is typically interrogated in the unfamiliar surroundings of a police station, is faced with several detectives who want to get a confession, is not free to go, and is alone, cut off from anyone he or she knows. The ACLU

THE COMPANION CASES

The Supreme Court heard Miranda's appeal along with three other cases involving police interrogation of indigent suspects in custody. One of those cases was *Vignera v. New York*. The New York City police arrested Michael Vignera on suspicion of robbing a dress shop. He was interrogated for eight hours at three police stations before he signed a confession. The police did not tell him that he had the right not to answer their questions. His conviction was affirmed by the New York Court of Appeals.

Another case to be heard with Miranda's was *California v. Stewart*. The Los Angeles police arrested Roy Stewart for first-degree murder and robbery and held him in custody for five days. After nine interrogation sessions, Stewart confessed. The record of the case did not indicate whether the police had advised him of his rights. He was convicted in the trial court, but the California Supreme Court had reversed the conviction. It was the prosecution's appeal of that reversal that the U.S. Supreme Court heard.

The third case was *Westover v. United States*. Unlike the other three cases, this case came from federal court, not from a state court. The Kansas City, Missouri, police arrested Carl Westover for two local robberies. In two interrogation sessions, he denied any role in the crimes. One day after the arrest, the FBI took custody of Westover in connection with two bank robberies in California. After a few hours of interrogation, Westover confessed to the bank robberies. Like Miranda, Westover signed a written confession on a form that had a printed paragraph simply stating that the police had advised him of his rights. His conviction in U.S. District Court was affirmed by a U.S. court of appeals, and the next step was to appeal to the Supreme Court.

argued that "there is a need to provide the presence of someone at interrogation in whom the subject can confide and who will bolster his confidence." [30] The ACLU's reasoning indicated that the presence of counsel at interrogation (appointed, if need be) is necessary to protect the right to remain silent. The attorney could advise the suspect of his or her right to remain silent, be an ally in the interrogation room, and give him or her the strength to resist police efforts to obtain a confession. These benefits would help suspects who were innocent of any crimes as well as suspects who had indeed committed the crime under investigation.

None of these amicus briefs referred specifically to Miranda's case or to the three companion cases. They focused on the larger legal issues presented by the cases. Ernesto Miranda's case had grown from a simple rape prosecution in Arizona into a case that the U.S. Supreme Court would use to address the constitutional rights of criminal suspects in police custody.

The Court Hears Oral Argument

After all the briefs have been submitted by the lawyers and read by the justices, the Supreme Court hears oral argument of the case in its majestic marble courthouse, just across the street from the Capitol in Washington, D.C. On February 28, 1966, all the lawyers in Ernesto Miranda's case assembled in the courtroom. The nine justices of the Supreme Court came into the courtroom at 10:00 A.M. and took their seats on the high bench in the front of the room. Chief Justice Earl Warren sat in the middle chair. Sitting to his left and right respectively, were Justices Hugo Black and William O. Douglas. Chief Justice Warren and Justices Black and Douglas had led the Supreme Court's recent movement to require state courts to protect the rights of criminal defendants as part of the due process guaranteed by the Fourteenth Amendment. Younger justices who often agreed with these three elders were William Brennan and Abe Fortas. The other four justices—Tom Clark, John Harlan, Potter Stewart, and Byron White—were less likely to expand the rights of state criminal defendants under the Fourteenth Amendment.

Justice Tom Clark, pictured here shortly after his 1949 appointment to the Supreme Court, opposed the expansion of rights for criminal defendants.

In 1964, Chief Justice Warren and Justices Black, Douglas, and Brennan had all voted to reverse the defendant's conviction in *Escobedo v. Illinois*. They had been joined then by Justice Arthur Goldberg, who left the Court in 1965 to become the U.S. ambassador to the United Nations. Justice Fortas had been appointed by President Lyndon B. Johnson to replace Justice Goldberg. Legal experts thought that Justice Fortas's views on interrogations were similar to those of Justice Goldberg. The lawyers for the four defendants now before the Supreme Court wanted to convince the nine justices that their cases were similar to *Escobedo* and thus should result in a similar decision.

Flynn's Argument on Behalf of Miranda

The Supreme Court heard Miranda's case first. John Flynn began his argument on behalf of Miranda. The Court allowed him (and each of the other lawyers) thirty minutes to address the Court. He spoke first about the facts of the case, emphasizing Miranda's poverty, lack of education, and psychological problems. He then argued that the Arizona Supreme Court had "emasculated" the ruling in *Escobedo* by holding that it applied only to suspects who ask to consult a lawyer and can afford to pay one. He argued that the spirit of *Escobedo* required that poor and

DIFFERENT ARGUMENTS
BY DIFFERENT LAWYERS

In their brief for *Miranda*, John Flynn and John Frank made a three-point argument as to why their client was entitled to a new trial. The first point was that the Fourteenth Amendment to the U.S. Constitution required the State of Arizona to give Miranda due process of law in the criminal proceedings against him. The second point was that due process includes the right to counsel guaranteed to criminal defendants by the Sixth Amendment. The third point was that the right to counsel, which had been extended to suspects under custodial interrogation in the *Escobedo* decision, required that a lawyer be appointed to advise indigent suspects during custodial interrogation. No such lawyer had been appointed for Ernesto Miranda.

Two other lawyers in the interrogation cases made different arguments that had an effect on the reasoning that the Supreme Court used in its final decision. The amicus curiae brief of the ACLU, written primarily by law professor Anthony Amsterdam, used the same first point, that the state must provide due process of law to criminal defendants. However, its second point was that due process includes the right not to be compelled to incriminate oneself, guaranteed to criminal defendants by the Fifth Amendment. The ACLU's resulting third point was that, for indigent suspects under interrogation, the right not to be compelled to incriminate oneself could be made effective only by the appointment of counsel to advise them.

Victor Earle was the attorney who represented the defendant in *Vignera v. New York*. He argued the same first two points as did the ACLU, but his third point was that the police had to give certain warnings of rights to suspects before they could interrogate them. The Supreme Court incorporated elements from the various briefs in reaching its decision. It based its decision on the Fifth Amendment, as the ACLU brief argued. It required the appointment of counsel for indigent suspects, as the *Miranda* brief argued. It also required the giving of warnings of rights prior to interrogation, as the *Vignera* brief argued.

---

uneducated suspects have lawyers appointed to enable them to know of their right to remain silent and to exercise that right.

During an attorney's allotted thirty minutes, the justices often interrupt to ask questions. Justice Stewart, one of the dissenters in *Escobedo*, questioned Flynn about what rights a suspect has at the interrogation stage. Like the ACLU brief, Flynn relied on both the right to counsel and the right to remain silent:

MR. JUSTICE STEWART: Well, again, I don't mean to quibble, and I apologize, but I think it's first important to define what those rights are—what his rights under the constitution are at that point. He can't be advised of his rights unless somebody knows what those rights are.

MR. FLYNN: Precisely my point. And the only person that can adequately advise a person like Ernesto Miranda is a lawyer.

MR. JUSTICE STEWART: And what would a lawyer advise him that his rights were?

MR. FLYNN: That he had a right not to incriminate himself; that he had the right not to make any statement; that he had a right to be free from further questioning by the police department; that he had the right, at the ultimate time, to be represented adequately by counsel in court; and that if he was too indigent or too poor to employ counsel, the state would furnish him counsel.[31]

A few minutes later, Justice White asked Flynn whether Miranda was covered by the Fifth Amendment, which provides that no person "shall be compelled in any criminal case to be a witness against himself":

MR. JUSTICE STEWART: Is there any claim in this case that this confession was compelled—was involuntary?

MR. FLYNN: No, Your Honor.

MR. JUSTICE STEWART: None at all?

MR. FLYNN: None at all.

MR. JUSTICE WHITE: Do you mean that there is no question that he was not compelled to give evidence against himself?

MR. FLYNN: We have raised no question that he was compelled to give this statement, in the sense that anyone forced him to do it by coercion, by threats, by promises, or compulsion of that kind.

MR. JUSTICE WHITE: "Of that kind"? Was it voluntary, or wasn't it?

MR. FLYNN: Voluntary in the sense that the man, at a time without knowledge of his rights—

MR. JUSTICE WHITE: Do you claim that his Fifth Amendment rights were violated?

MR. FLYNN: I would say that his Fifth Amendment right was violated, to the extent—

MR. JUSTICE WHITE: Because he was compelled to do it?

MR. FLYNN: Because he was compelled to do it?

MR. JUSTICE WHITE: That's what the Amendment says.

MR. FLYNN: Yes, to the extent that he was, number one, too poor to exercise it, and number two, mentally abnormal. . . .

MR. JUSTICE WHITE: But in all the circumstances—I'm just trying to find out if you claim that his Fifth Amendment rights were being violated. If they were, it must be because he was compelled to do it, under all circumstances.

MR. FLYNN: I would say that as a result of a lack of knowledge, or for lack of a better term "failure to advise," the denial of the right to counsel at the stage in the proceeding when he most certainly needed it, that this

During the appeal, Supreme Court Justice Byron White questioned whether Miranda's Fifth Amendment rights were violated or whether he voluntarily confessed to his crimes.

could, in and of itself—and certainly in most police inter-rogations—constitute compulsion.[32]

Justice White's questions focused on a weak point in Flynn's argument. Flynn stated that the police had not compelled Miranda to confess, meaning that the police had not beaten or threatened him. Justice White then pointed out that the Fifth Amendment provides that "no person . . . shall be compelled in any criminal case to be a witness against himself." His point was that if the police had not compelled Miranda to confess, then the Fifth Amendment did not apply to this case. Flynn quickly told the justices that Miranda had indeed been compelled to confess because of the failure of the police to advise him of his right to an attorney. After a few more questions, Flynn made some con-cluding remarks and sat down.

Nelson's Argument on Behalf of the State of Arizona

Nelson then began his presentation on behalf of the State of Ari-zona. He argued that Miranda was not insane when he was ar-rested and that he knew of his right not to answer questions by the interrogating police officers. Nelson responded to Justice Fortas's statement that "I suppose it's quite arguable that Mi-randa, this petitioner here, was entitled to a warning":

> MR. NELSON: It's arguable. I have extensively argued the fact that he wasn't of such a nature, as an individual who because of his mental condition or his educational background, as to require any more than he got. In other words, I'm saying that he got every warning, except the right—the specific warning of the right to counsel. He didn't have counsel. Counsel wasn't specifically denied to him, on the basis of a request to retain counsel. The only possible thing that happened to Mr. Miranda that, in my light, assuming that he had the capability of un-derstanding at all, is the fact that he did not get the spe-cific warning of his right to counsel.[33]

Nelson stuck to his position that whatever warnings must be given to a suspect varies according to the facts of the individual case.

Gary Nelson, assistant attorney general for the State of Arizona, argued that Miranda had been sufficiently warned of his rights at the time of his arrest and subsequent interrogation.

Nelson predicted the undesirable result that "when counsel is introduced at interrogation, interrogation ceases immediately." [34] He argued that the appointment of counsel at interrogations would reduce the number of confessions that the police would obtain from guilty suspects. Justice Black asked whether that result is exactly what the right to remain silent under the Fifth Amendment intended. Nelson insisted that the presence of counsel for a suspect would needlessly hinder police interrogations and was not a required element of due process of law.

The Other Oral Arguments

With the end of Nelson's argument, the Court had heard from both Miranda and from the State of Arizona. For the remainder of Monday, all of Tuesday, and part of Wednesday, the Court continued to hear oral arguments on the issue of interrogations. The lawyers in the other three cases about interrogations all made oral arguments discussing the rights of suspects under interrogation in police custody. Lawyers representing the twenty-nine state attorneys general and the National District Attorneys Association also addressed the Court. The other amicus curiae, the ACLU, did not make an oral argument.

By Wednesday afternoon, March 2, 1966, the arguments were over. Most of them had discussed general questions of law as it relates to police interrogations. There had been little discussion of Lois Ann Jameson, of Ernesto Miranda, or of the people involved in the other three cases. Although the outcome would affect those people, the justices would meet and discuss the greater issues of constitutional law that affect all persons in this country.

Chapter 6

The Supreme Court Decision

O N MONDAY, JUNE 13, 1966, the nine Supreme Court justices took their seats at the bench for the last time before the Court's summer vacation. It had been over three months since the oral arguments in Ernesto Miranda's case and the other three interrogation cases. After many conferences and much discussion among themselves, the justices were ready to announce their decision. A crowded courtroom listened.

In announcing a decision in the courtroom, the justice who writes the majority decision for the Court usually states the outcome briefly, leaving the legal analysis for interested people to read in the Court's written decision. In this case, however, Chief Justice Warren read his entire written decision in the four cases. It took him about one hour to read it, with emotion sometimes rising in his voice. The bottom line was that Miranda and the three defendants in the other cases were all entitled to new trials. Although each of the four had confessed under police interrogation, the Supreme Court, by a vote of five to four, ruled that the confessions were invalid because the police had failed to protect the right of suspects not to incriminate themselves. Several times, however, Chief Justice Warren emphasized that the new procedures that police would have to follow would not hamper effective law enforcement.

It had not been an easy decision to reach. In his written decision, Chief Justice Warren spoke only for himself and four

CHIEF JUSTICE EARL WARREN

Earl Warren was no stranger to the criminal justice system when he became chief justice in 1953. He had been an assistant state prosecutor for Alameda County in California from 1920 to 1925. Alameda County was a large county, in both population and area, and Oakland was its largest city. Earl Warren became the chief prosecutor for the county in 1925 and held that job until 1938. As a prosecutor, he became familiar with the rigorous interrogations suspects would sometimes undergo. He developed a reputation for fairness and honesty in how he ran the prosecutor's office.

In 1938, Warren successfully ran as the Republican candidate for California attorney general, the head legal officer for the state government. It was while Warren was California's attorney general that President Franklin D. Roosevelt ordered the internment of Japanese Americans early in World War II. Warren took a large role in carrying out this order, and the Japanese Americans stayed in the internment camps for most of the war. Late in life, Warren expressed regret for his participation in the evacuation and internment.

Chief Justice Earl Warren poses beside an impressive oil portrait of himself in this 1963 photograph.

Earl Warren won the 1942 election for governor of California and was re-elected twice. He supported progressive measures such as improved schools and public health care. In 1948, he was the Republican candidate for vice president of the United States, going down to defeat as President Harry Truman, the Democratic candidate, narrowly defeated Governor Thomas E. Dewey of New York, Warren's running mate on the Republican ticket.

In 1952, Earl Warren sought the Republican nomination for president. General Dwight D. Eisenhower, a hero of World War II, won that nomination and was elected president. Warren supported Eisenhower in the general election. When Chief Justice Fred Vinson died on September 8, 1953, President Eisenhower nominated Warren to take his place on the Supreme Court.

other justices. Two of the dissenting justices (Justices Clark and Harlan) also read their written opinions with emotion in their voices. In all, four of the nine justices voted to affirm Miranda's convictions. By a slim one-vote margin, Ernesto Miranda would have another chance to regain his freedom. By that same margin, the Supreme Court greatly changed the rules governing police interrogation.

The Majority Decision

Chief Justice Warren's decision had the support of Justices Black, Douglas, Brennan, and Fortas. These five justices ruled that the due process clause of the Fourteenth Amendment re-quires the police to follow certain procedures before confessions

made under custodial interrogation can be used in court. From that point on, police interrogation of sus-pects would be governed by the Supreme Court's written decision in *Miranda v. Arizona*.

To understand the decision of the Supreme Court, it is best to read certain parts of its written

Justices Abe Fortas (top), Hugo Black (center), William Douglas (bottom), and William Brennan formed the majority in support of Chief Justice Warren's ruling in the Miranda *case.*

JUSTICES BLACK AND DOUGLAS

Four justices joined Chief Justice Warren in declaring new minimum standards governing police interrogation of suspects in their custody. Two of them were Justices Hugo Black and William O. Douglas, both of whom had joined the Supreme Court in the 1930s. President Franklin D. Roosevelt nominated them for the Court because they had been supporters of the president's program known as the New Deal. With a severe economic depression plaguing the country when he took office in 1933, President Roosevelt and Congress increased the power of the federal government to regulate economic affairs throughout the country. The Supreme Court had declared some of that legislation unconstitutional in the mid-1930s. When several seats on the Court became vacant in the late 1930s, President Roosevelt nominated men who were likely to uphold the New Deal legislation. Justice Black was a senator from Alabama when he joined the Court in 1937. Justice Douglas was chairman of the Securities and Exchange Commission, a new federal agency regulating the stock market, when he joined the Court in 1939. As justices, both men did indeed vote to approve legislation expanding federal regulatory power.

Justices Black and Douglas also became the leading civil libertarians on the Supreme Court during their long careers there. They consistently voted to increase safeguards for individuals under the Fifth and Fourteenth Amendments to the U.S. Constitution. Although Chief Justice Warren is usually given credit for the Supreme Court's expansion of the rights of criminal defendants during his leadership of the Court, Justices Black and Douglas had fought for such changes for years before Chief Justice Warren joined the Court.

---

decision. The following paragraph is an introduction to the decision:

> The cases before us raise questions which go to the roots of our concepts of American criminal jurisprudence: the restraints society must observe consistent with the Federal Constitution in prosecuting individuals for crime. More specifically, we deal with the admissibility of statements obtained from an individual who is subjected to custodial police interrogation and the necessity for procedures which assure that the individual is accorded his privilege under the Fifth Amendment to the Constitution not to be compelled to incriminate himself.[35]

This paragraph announces that the decision will not just resolve the fates of Miranda and the three other defendants but will set rules to govern interrogations of all suspects in police custody. It also states that the Court was deciding the four cases on the basis of the right not to incriminate oneself, protected in federal cases by the Fifth Amendment and in state cases by the due process clause of the Fourteenth Amendment. The Court did not primarily rely on the right to counsel guaranteed by the Sixth Amendment, despite the urging of Miranda's lawyers.

Near the start of the written decision, Chief Justice Warren summarized the Court's ruling:

> Our holding will be spelled out with some specificity in the pages which follow but briefly stated it is this: the prosecution may not use statements, either exculpatory or inculpatory, stemming from custodial interrogation of the defendant unless it demonstrates the use of procedural safeguards effective to secure the privilege against self-incrimination. By custodial interrogation, we mean questioning initiated by law enforcement officers after a person has been taken into custody or otherwise deprived of his freedom of action in any significant way.[36]

In other words, nothing a suspect says while under interrogation in police custody can be used by prosecutors unless police take steps to protect the suspect's right against self-incrimination.

Chief Justice Warren then stated the "procedural safeguards" that the police would have to use:

> Prior to any questioning, the person must be warned that he has a right to remain silent, that any statement he does make may be used as evidence against him, and that he has a right to the presence of an attorney, either retained or appointed.[37]

The Court then held that if the suspect refuses to answer any questions or asks to consult with an attorney, the police must stop the questioning. Although a suspect can decide to answer police questions, he or she must first understand the rights to remain silent and to consult with an attorney and must give those rights up voluntarily.

Protecting the Right to Remain Silent

Although Miranda and the other three defendants had not been threatened or beaten before they confessed, the Court nevertheless ruled that the psychological pressure of custodial interrogation, made without warnings of rights, was a form of unconstitutional compulsion. The Court explained that all four cases before it involved "incommunicado interrogation of individuals in a police-dominated atmosphere, resulting in self-incriminating statements without full warnings of constitutional rights." The questioning of a person in police custody, separated from friends and family in a strange environment, "exacts a heavy toll on individual liberty and trades on the weakness of individuals." [38] The Court wanted to impose rules that would enable suspects (guilty or innocent) to remain silent under interrogation if they so chose.

As to warnings, Chief Justice Warren stated that "at the outset, if a person in custody is to be subjected to interrogation, he must first be informed in clear and unequivocal terms that he has the right to remain silent." He stated that "such a warning is an absolute prerequisite in overcoming the inherent pressures of the interrogation atmosphere." In addition, "the warning of the right to remain silent must be accompanied by the explanation that anything said can and will be used against the individual in court." [39]

As to the right to have a lawyer present during the interrogation process, the Court held that "the right to have counsel present at the interrogation is indispensable to the protection of the Fifth Amendment privilege under the system we delineate today." [40] Moreover, the police have to inform suspects of this right to have an attorney with them during interrogation. This right to counsel during interrogation was first set forth by the Supreme Court in its 1964 decision in *Escobedo v. Illinois*, where it was based on the right to counsel protected by the Sixth Amendment. In *Miranda*, however, the Supreme Court found the same right as part of the right not to incriminate oneself, guaranteed by the Fifth Amendment.

As to indigent suspects, the Court held that "if an individual indicates that he wishes the assistance of counsel before any interrogation occurs, the authorities cannot rationally ignore or deny his request on the basis that the individual does not have or cannot afford a retained attorney."[41] This is the argument that Miranda's attorneys had voiced from the beginning. In the future, the police would have to arrange for appointed counsel to advise a poor suspect whom they wished to interrogate.

For the first time, the Court imposed on the federal and state governments the duty to provide an attorney during interrogation for suspects who cannot afford to hire one. The Court noted that the Congress and the states were free to devise different systems to protect the defendant's right to remain silent, provided that such an alternative system was "at least as effective in apprising accused persons of their right of silence and in assuring a continuous opportunity to exercise it."[42] In the years since the *Miranda* decision, however, neither Congress nor any state has devised an acceptable alternative system.

At the end of the written decision, the Court addressed the facts of the four cases before it. As to Miranda, the Court reversed his conviction and stated the reasons:

> From the testimony of the officers and by the admission of [the prosecution], it is clear that Miranda was not in any way apprised of his right to consult with an attorney and to have one present during the interrogation, nor was his right not to be compelled to incriminate himself effectively protected in any other manner. Without these warnings the statements were inadmissible. The mere fact that he signed a statement which contained a typed-in clause stating that he had "full knowledge" of his "legal rights" does not approach the knowing and intelligent waiver required to relinquish constitutional rights.[43]

The Court similarly held that the confessions in the three other cases were also invalid.

The Dissenting Opinions

Of the nine justices of the Supreme Court, four of them dissented from (disagreed with) Chief Justice Warren's written decision. Justices Clark, Harlan, Stewart, and White all voted to affirm (keep in place) Miranda's conviction. Justices Clark, Harlan, and White all wrote opinions explaining how they viewed the case. Justice Stewart did not write his own opinion, but he agreed with the opinions of Justices Harlan and White.

Justice Clark's written opinion was the shortest. He stated that the new rules adopted by the Court were not required by the Constitution. In his view, the rule governing confessions should continue to be that they can be received into evidence at a trial if, in light of all circumstances, they are voluntarily made. Justice Clark voted to affirm the convictions of Miranda and two of the other defendants, but he voted to overturn the conviction of the fourth defendant on the ground that his confession might have been involuntary.

Justice Harlan voted to uphold all the confessions as voluntarily made. He criticized the Court's majority decision because it would make it difficult to obtain confessions. He wrote that "the thrust of the new rules is to negate all pressures, to reinforce the nervous or ignorant suspect, and ultimately to discourage any confession at all." He also stated that "the Court's unspoken assumption that any pressure violates the privilege is not supported by the precedents and it has failed to show why the Fifth Amendment prohibits that relatively mild pressure the Due Process Clause permits."[44] In his view, the due process clause of the Fourteenth Amendment required only that confessions not be involuntary in the sense that they are the product of threats or force. Neither warnings nor appointed counsel was necessary as a constitutional matter.

In his dissenting opinion, Justice Harlan stated that "police questioning allowable under due process precedents may inherently entail some pressure on the suspect and may seek advantage in his ignorance or weakness." Prior to the *Miranda* decision, "the role of the Constitution has been only to sift out undue pressure, not to assure spontaneous confessions." In Justice

THE DISSENTING JUSTICES

Four justices dissented from Chief Justice Warren's opinion for the Court in *Miranda*. Justice Tom C. Clark grew up in Texas and joined the U.S. Justice Department in 1937. As an assistant attorney general, he had helped the U.S. Army evacuate Japanese Americans from the West Coast and intern them in camps in 1941 and 1942. He became the U.S. attorney general under President Harry S. Truman, who nominated him to the Supreme Court in 1949. He would resign from the Court in 1967, when his son became attorney general under President Lyndon B. Johnson.

Justice John M. Harlan was nominated to the Court by President Eisenhower in 1954. His grandfather had also been a justice of the U.S. Supreme Court. Justice Harlan often opposed Justice Black by urging that the Court not expand the rights of individuals. He argued that if rights were to be expanded, it was proper for the elected legislatures to make that decision, not appointed judges. He and Justice Black were fast friends, and they both left the Court because of illness within a week of each other in September 1971. Both of them died before the end of that year.

Justice Potter Stewart joined the Court in 1958, when he was only forty-three years of age. He grew up in Cincinnati, where his father had been mayor. He served on the Court for twenty-three years before he resigned in 1981. He usually sought out the middle position on most legal questions. In criminal cases, however, he favored the prosecution more often than Chief Justice Warren and Justices Black, Douglas, and Brennan.

Similar to Justice Stewart in voting was Justice Byron R. White, nominated by President John F. Kennedy in 1963. Justice White was better known to the public as Whizzer White, an All-American halfback for the University of Colorado and a two-time rushing leader of the National Football League. He had served with distinction in World War II, graduated with honors from Yale Law School, and was a highly ranked official in the Justice Department under President Kennedy.

Harlan's opinion, the new rules would unnecessarily hinder law enforcement:

> What the Court largely ignores is that its rules impair, if they will not eventually serve wholly to frustrate, an instrument of law enforcement that has long and quite reasonably been thought worth the price paid for it. There can be little doubt that the Court's new code would

markedly decrease the number of confessions. To warn the suspect that he may remain silent and remind him that his confession may be used in court are minor obstructions. To require also an express waiver by the suspect and an end to questioning whenever he demurs must heavily handicap questioning. And to suggest or provide counsel for the suspect simply invites the end of the interrogation.

Justice Harlan thought that "the Court portrays the evils of normal police questioning in terms which I think are exaggerated." [45]

Justice Harlan continued to criticize the Court's decision as he addressed the facts of Miranda's case:

Mr. Miranda's oral and written confessions are now held inadmissible under the Court's new rules. One is entitled to feel astonished that the Constitution can be read to produce this result. These confessions were obtained during brief, daytime questioning conducted by two officers and unmarked by any of the traditional indicia of coercion. They assured a conviction for a brutal and unsettling crime, for which the police had and quite possibly could obtain little evidence other than the victim's identifications, evidence which is frequently unreliable. There was, in sum, a legitimate purpose, no perceptible unfairness, and certainly little risk of injustice in the interrogation. Yet the resulting confessions and the responsible course of police practice they represent, are to be sacrificed to the Court's own finespun conception of fairness which I seriously doubt is shared by many thinking citizens in this country.

He concluded by stating that "I would adhere to the due process test and reject the new requirements inaugurated by the court." [46]

Justice White also voted to uphold all four convictions. He began his written opinion by stating that "the proposition that the privilege against self-incrimination forbids in-custody interrogation without the warnings specified in the majority opinion and without a clear waiver of counsel has no significant support

Byron White, one of the dissenting Supreme Court justices in the Miranda *decision, feared that the Court's decision would hinder law enforcement and provide a loophole for offenders.*

in the history of the privilege or in the language of the Fifth Amendment." [47] He believed that the Fifth Amendment forbade only self-incrimination that was "compelled" and that a confession made out of ignorance of rights was not compelled.

Justice White strongly criticized the effect he believed the new rules would have on law enforcement:

> In some unknown number of cases the Court's rule will return a killer, a rapist or other criminal to the streets and to the environment which produced him, to repeat his crime whenever it pleases him. As a consequence, there will not be a gain, but a loss, in human dignity. The real concern is not the unfortunate consequences of this new decision on the criminal law as an abstract, disembodied series of authoritative proscriptions, but the impact on those who rely on the public authority for protection and who without it can only engage in violent self-help with guns, knives and the help of their neighbors similarly

inclined. There is, of course, a saving factor: the next victims are uncertain, unnamed and unrepresented in this case.[48]

Despite these fears, the decision of the Court (written by Chief Justice Warren) was now the law of the land.

The Immediate Reaction

The Supreme Court decision was front-page news in the nation's newspapers. On June 14, 1966, the biggest headline on page one of the *New York Times* read "High Court Puts New Curb on Powers of the Police to Interrogate Suspects." [49] On that same morning, the *Washington Post* had a large headline, running across the top of page one, reading "High Court Curbs Police Questioning." [50] The *Miranda* decision had become a matter of public interest and would spark a public debate on whether the Supreme Court was improperly hindering the police in the effort to solve crimes and prosecute criminals.

As one might expect, prosecutors and police officials criticized the decision bitterly. New York City police commissioner Howard R. Leary held a press conference on the day after the *Miranda* decision was issued. He said that because of the decision, "it's quite possible that a great number of persons who are in fact guilty will not be successfully prosecuted." He predicted that "we just won't be able to offer the district attorneys and the courts as much evidence." He complained further that "all decisions from the Supreme Court recently always favor the accused and the defendants, and are greatly concerned with their rights. How far and how long are the rights of the accused to be considered, with little regard for the rights of the victim?" Commissioner Leary tried to be optimistic, stating that "it looks very grim, but in the long run it may have good effects because now you'll have to come up with more scientific techniques to solve crime." [51]

Other police officials and prosecutors harshly criticized the *Miranda* decision. Boston police commissioner Edmund L. McNamara complained that "criminal trials no longer will be a search for truth, but a search for technical error." Philadelphia police commissioner Edward J. Bell stated that the new rules on interrogation "protect the guilty."[52] Maricopa County attorney Robert K. Corbin, the head of the office that prosecuted Miranda, said, "God help us. God help the public. I sincerely mean this."[53]

Some other reactions to the decision were positive. Lawyers interested in protecting the civil rights of criminal suspects were, of course, very happy. David G. Bress, the top federal prosecutor in the District of Columbia courts, said that "eventually the changes have to sharpen police investigations in other areas and the public will benefit."[54] Charles E. Moylan Jr., a respected prosecutor in Baltimore, stated that the *Miranda* decision would, in the long run, "be good for law enforcement and make for a better brand of justice."[55]

These early reactions were just the start of a debate that would continue for years.

Chapter 7

After the *Miranda* Decision

THE *MIRANDA* DECISION WAS very important for Ernesto Miranda, but it also had major consequences for the country at large. It changed the way that the police do their business. For the first time, the Bill of Rights of the U.S. Constitution reached into police interrogation rooms and required that the rights of all suspects (innocent or guilty) against self-incrimination be protected. In the decades since the decision, the Supreme Court has had to wrestle with applying the *Miranda* decision to all sorts of different factual situations. For Ernesto Miranda himself, the decision gave him the opportunity for a new trial on the charges of kidnapping and raping Lois Ann Jameson.

Police Adjustments to the *Miranda* Decision

Despite the complaints of police officials when the Supreme Court's decision was announced, police departments around the United States went about the necessary task of complying with the *Miranda* decision. Although the police had previously conducted interrogations without much supervision from courts, specific court-made rules now limited what could be done in the isolated rooms of the police station. Officers and detectives would have to learn the warnings that the Supreme Court said were necessary. Different police departments used different words, but the warnings always were something like this: "You have the right to remain silent. Anything you say can and will be used against you in a court of law. You have the right to talk to a lawyer and have him present with you while you are being questioned. If you cannot afford to hire a lawyer, one will be appointed to represent you before any questioning, if you wish one."

These warnings were printed on forms called Miranda cards. At first, police officers and detectives carried these cards so that they could read the warnings. But they soon learned the warnings by heart. Police departments then printed the warnings on forms that suspects could sign if they wished to waive their rights and speak to the questioners.

Miranda warnings have only slightly reduced the number of confessions. Studies indicate that more than 80 percent of suspects waive their rights and talk to the police without an attorney present. A large majority of those who answer questions wind up confessing or making statements that incriminate themselves. Several reasons may explain this phenomenon. Despite the warnings about rights, it is very intimidating for someone to be in custody at a police station, surrounded by armed officers

Following the Supreme Court's decision in Miranda, *police departments throughout the country began providing suspects with Miranda cards and forms like this one from the San Francisco Police Department.*

DEFENDANT	LOCATION

SPECIFIC WARNING REGARDING INTERROGATIONS

1. YOU HAVE THE RIGHT TO REMAIN SILENT.

2. ANYTHING YOU SAY CAN AND WILL BE USED AGAINST YOU IN A COURT OF LAW.

3. YOU HAVE THE RIGHT TO TALK TO A LAWYER AND HAVE HIM PRESENT WITH YOU WHILE YOU ARE BEING QUESTIONED.

4. IF YOU CANNOT AFFORD TO HIRE A LAWYER ONE WILL BE APPOINTED TO REPRESENT YOU BEFORE ANY QUESTIONING, IF YOU WISH ONE.

SIGNATURE OF DEFENDANT	DATE
WITNESS	TIME

☐ REFUSED SIGNATURE   SAN FRANCISCO POLICE DEPARTMENT   PR.9.1.4

Even with Miranda warnings, many suspects feel intimidated while in police custody.

who believe that that person has committed a crime. A suspect in that vulnerable position may want to please the interrogators in hopes of receiving less severe punishment. Talking, rather than keeping silent, would seem to be the way to please the interrogators. Police are now trained in techniques to convince suspects to talk with them. For example, a questioner may try to establish a friendly bond with a suspect. Some interrogators tell suspects that they must talk right away in order to make a deal for lesser charges.

When suspects state that they do not want to answer questions, the interrogators are supposed to stop their questions immediately. They usually do stop, but some detectives continue questioning anyway. These officers realize that they cannot use any confession obtained in this manner in court. Nevertheless, they hope to get clues from the suspects to help them prove the case. These violations of the Miranda rules may become rarer as interrogations are videotaped, a new practice that is becoming more common with police departments.

All in all, the *Miranda* case has hindered the police very little in the area of interrogations. Even in cases in which confessions cannot be obtained, new methods of detection, like DNA analysis, help prosecutors achieve convictions.

Politics and *Miranda*

The *Miranda* decision was only one in a series of cases in which the Supreme Court expanded the rights of criminal suspects and defendants, but it became a symbol that politicians could use to convince people to vote for them. During the summer and fall of 1968, former U.S. vice president Richard M. Nixon, the Republican candidate for president, made "law and order" a major issue in his campaign. He criticized the Supreme Court for its decisions in major criminal cases, including *Miranda*. He promised that if he were elected president, he would appoint a chief justice who would favor the police more than the soon-to-retire Earl Warren did.

Richard Nixon won the election and took office in January 1969. Chief Justice Warren stayed on the job until the summer of 1969. President Nixon then nominated Warren Burger, a judge on the U.S. Court of Appeals in the District of Columbia, to be the new chief justice. Judge Burger had stated in a 1967 speech that the Supreme Court's criminal decisions, including *Miranda*, had made it too hard for society to catch and punish criminals. He said that "it is often very difficult to convict even those who are plainly guilty." [56] The Senate confirmed the nomination, and Chief Justice Burger took charge of the Supreme Court when it came back from its summer vacation in October 1969.

In the years since then, political views on *Miranda* have been relatively consistent. Politicians with a more liberal philosophy support the *Miranda* decision, applauding the protection it gives to suspects who are generally poor, uneducated, and of a racial or ethnic minority. Those with a more conservative philosophy criticize the *Miranda* decision, arguing that the police should be able to get confessions from guilty suspects who are ignorant of their rights. The debate continues to this day.

THE WARREN COURT BREAKS UP

When Chief Justice Warren led the U.S. Supreme Court in the first half of 1969, there were six justices on the Court who frequently voted to expand the rights of criminal defendants in the state and federal courts. These six included Chief Justice Warren and Justices Hugo Black, William Douglas, William Brennan, Abe Fortas, and Thurgood Marshall. All but Justice Marshall had joined in the Court's decision in *Miranda* in 1966. Justice Marshall had joined the Court in 1967, replacing Justice Tom Clark, who had dissented in *Miranda*. Still on the Court in early 1969 were the other three *Miranda* dissenters, Justices John Harlan, Potter Stewart, and Byron White. The liberal wing of the Warren Court was in full control, with a usual 6-3 voting edge.

Things began to change in the spring of 1969 with the resignation of Justice Fortas. That summer, Chief Justice Warren's retirement took effect, and he was replaced by President Nixon's nominee, Warren Burger. The new chief justice held a more conservative legal philosophy, believing that the Court should not expand the legal rights of criminal defendants. To fill Justice Fortas's seat, the Senate confirmed Justice Harry Blackmun in 1970. He also had a conservative legal philosophy, at least in his first years on the Court.

In the summer of 1971, both Justice Black and Justice Harlan resigned from the Court because of bad health. President Nixon nomiated (and the Senate confirmed) Lewis Powell and William Rehnquist to the Court. They also held conservative legal views on the issue of expanding the rights of criminal defendants.

Thus, between 1969 and 1972, the Supreme Court had a substantial change in its membership and philosophy. The 6-3 liberal majority under Chief Justice Warren had turned into a 6-3 conservative majority under Chief Justice Burger. No longer would the Supreme Court regularly issue groundbreaking decisions increasing the procedural protections for criminal defendants.

Later Supreme Court Decisions

Chief Justice Warren Burger led the Supreme Court from 1969 to 1986. Although some other justices with a conservative philosophy joined the Court during those years, the Court never overruled the *Miranda* decision. Indeed, in a 1980 case, Chief Justice Burger wrote that "the meaning of *Miranda* has become reasonably clear and law enforcement practices have adjusted to its strictures. I would neither overrule *Miranda*, disparage it, nor extend it at this late date."[57] However, the Supreme Court made several decisions in the Burger years that limited the *Miranda* decision or chipped away at its force.

In 1971, two years after Chief Justice Burger took office, the Supreme Court decided the case of *Harris v. New York*. The defendant in that case was arrested for selling illegal drugs to an undercover police officer. He made some self-incriminating statements under interrogation, during which the police did not give him the warnings required by the *Miranda* decision. At trial, the defendant took the witness stand and denied selling drugs to the officer. On cross-examination, the prosecution confronted him with his self-incriminatory statements made during interrogation. After he was found guilty, the defendant appealed, and his case made it to the U.S. Supreme Court. By a five-to-four vote, the Supreme Court affirmed the conviction. It held that the prosecution can use an inadmissible confession (under the *Miranda* rule) when a defendant testifies that he is innocent but has said differently to the police.

In 1974, the Supreme Court decided *Michigan v. Tucker*. The defendant in this case wanted to have the trial court exclude the testimony of a witness whom the police had learned about only from statements that the defendant made in an interrogation where he did not receive Miranda warnings. Eight of the nine justices voted to affirm the conviction. Justice William Rehnquist, appointed to the Court by President Nixon in 1972, wrote the Court's decision. Justice Rehnquist stated that the Miranda rules were not required by the U.S. Constitution itself but were only "recommended procedural safeguards"[58] to protect the Fifth Amendment right against self-incrimination. Justice Rehnquist seemed to some observers to be de-emphasizing the Miranda rules; it appeared that an overruling of *Miranda* perhaps lay in the future.

In 1984, the Court made a new exception to the interrogation rules in *New York v. Quarles*. In this case, a police officer chased the defendant, a rape suspect, into a supermarket. The officer lost sight of the defendant for a few seconds but caught him in the rear of the store. He handcuffed the defendant, felt an empty holster, and asked him where the gun was. The de-

William Rehnquist has served as chief justice of the Supreme Court since 1986. During his tenure the Court has continued to refine the complex issues first raised by Miranda v. Arizona.

fendant pointed to some empty cartons and said, "the gun is over there." The New York courts ruled that the defendant's statement and the gun could not be used as evidence at trial because the police officer asked him about the gun before giving him Miranda warnings. The Supreme Court reversed the state court decision and held that the prosecution could use the defendant's statement and the gun as evidence at trial. Justice Rehnquist wrote the Court's decision in a five-to-four decision that stated that, when public safety is at issue, the police can ask necessary questions before giving the Miranda warnings.

In 1986, upon Chief Justice Burger's retirement, President Ronald Reagan promoted Justice William Rehnquist to the position of chief justice. Chief Justice Rehnquist has now been at the head of the Supreme Court for over thirteen years, but the Court has not overruled *Miranda* during his time of leadership. Indeed, in 1993, in *Withrow v. Williams*, the Court reaffirmed the importance

THE SUPREME COURT TODAY

As the United States enters the first years of the twenty-first century, the Supreme Court takes a more conservative approach to criminal law and constitutional interpretation than it did under the leadership of Chief Justice Earl Warren. The Court today rarely expands the procedural rights of criminal defendants. It is more likely to expand the powers of the police and prosecution in fighting crime and convicting criminals. All of the significant rulings on criminal procedure made by the Supreme Court under Chief Justice Warren, however, remain in effect. Decisions in subsequent cases may have limited the effects of these rulings, but none have been overruled.

William Rehnquist, who joined the Court as an associate justice in 1972, was elevated to chief justice in 1986. He has a conservative legal philosophy and does not approve of expanding the rights of criminal defendants under the principle of due process. His closest allies on the Court are Justices Antonin Scalia and Clarence Thomas. The three of them are the most consistently conservative votes on issues of criminal law and other civil rights.

Another group of justices on the Court today is generally conservative, but not as conservative as Chief Justice Rehnquist and Justices Scalia and Thomas. This group includes Justices Sandra Day O'Connor, Anthony Kennedy, and David Souter. They sometimes join with the more moderate justices to reach decisions that the most conservative justices oppose.

The remainder of the Court's justices are considered moderate or liberal. This group includes Justices John Paul Stevens, Ruth Bader Ginsburg, and Stephen Breyer. They are more likely than the other justices to rule in favor of criminal defendants, but they are not nearly as likely to do so as were the justices led by Chief Justice Warren in the 1960s.

In the twenty-first century, new legal issues involving federal law will certainly arise. The Supreme Court will confront them. Everyone in the United States will, in one way or another, be affected by the decisions that the Court makes.

of the Miranda rules in protecting the right of a criminal defendant not to incriminate himself. Nevertheless, the Court has continued to narrow the force of the *Miranda* decision. For example, in the 1991 decision of *Arizona v. Fulminante*, the Court held that a criminal conviction supported by strong evidence can be affirmed even if the trial court erroneously allowed the jury to hear about a confession that was made without Miranda warnings. This extension of the "harmless error" principle to *Miranda* cases came in another five-to-four decision of the Court.

Miranda's Second Trial

The U.S. Supreme Court decision gave Ernesto Miranda new hope. It did not, however, immediately set him free. The Supreme Court had reversed his conviction, but the State of Arizona could again put him on trial as long as it did not use the confession. The state decided to proceed with a second trial in the Arizona Superior Court in Phoenix. Miranda stayed in prison while awaiting the new trial.

The lawyers and the judge were different from those at the first trial. John Flynn, the skilled criminal lawyer who argued Miranda's case at the U.S. Supreme Court, would represent him at trial, replacing Alvin Moore. Prosecuting the case for the State of Arizona was Robert Corbin, the top prosecutor for Maricopa County, replacing Lawrence Turoff, one of his assistants. The judge was Lawrence K. Wren, replacing Judge Yale McFate.

The trial started on February 15, 1967, and lasted nine days. On only one day, however, did the jury hear the testimony of witnesses. On the other eight days, the lawyers and the judge discussed and resolved various legal arguments about what evidence the jury should be allowed to see. Two witnesses testified for the prosecution. Lois Ann Jameson (now twenty-one, married, and a mother of two children) told the jury about how she had been abducted and raped almost four years before. On cross-examination, John Flynn got Jameson to make a serious concession. She admitted that she could not positively identify Miranda as the man who had attacked her in 1963. It had been a long time since the crime, and her identification had not been positive even shortly after the crime. With the victim unsure that Miranda was the rapist, and with his 1963 confession not admissible at trial, prospects were good that Miranda would be acquitted.

Twila Hoffman Comes Forward

The prosecution's other witness, however, was devastating to Miranda's case. That witness was Twila Hoffman, the woman with whom Miranda lived in 1963 and the mother of his daughter Cleopatra. Hoffman told the jury about her visit to Miranda in jail on March 16, 1963, only three days after his confession. Hoffman testified that Miranda told her then that he had in fact taken Lois Ann Jameson from the street and raped her. Miranda had asked Hoffman during that visit to contact Jameson and tell her that he would marry her if she would drop the charges. Hoffman had become very angry and refused to do that. Miranda then asked Hoffman to visit Jameson, to show her baby Cleopatra, and to ask her to drop the charges so that the baby's father could be free to support her. Hoffman had also refused to do that. Because Miranda had made this confession to Hoffman and not to the police, a warning of rights was not necessary, and the judge allowed the jury to hear about it.

Hoffman's testimony about the jailhouse confession convinced the jury to find Miranda guilty of rape and kidnapping. Judge Wren imposed a sentence of twenty to thirty years, the same sentence Judge McFate had imposed after the first trial.

The Second Trip up the Appellate Ladder

Now Ernesto Miranda would stay in prison with the same twenty- to thirty-year sentence that he had originally received. Despite Flynn's renewed efforts, no appellate court would come to his rescue. On February 7, 1969, the *Arizona Republic* carried a story with the headline of "Miranda's 2nd Trial for Rape Upheld by Arizona High Court." The article began by stating that "the Arizona Supreme Court yesterday morning affirmed the second rape and kidnapping conviction of Ernest A. Miranda, the Arizona State Prison inmate who made legal history when the U.S. Supreme Court upset his first conviction." Judge John Molloy, a Tucson judge sitting temporarily on the Arizona Supreme Court, wrote the court's decision. The *Republic* described the main issues that had been raised in the written briefs and the oral arguments:

> Convicted again upon retrial in Maricopa County Superior Court, Miranda contended on appeal to the Arizona Supreme Court that:

—His inadmissible confession to police prompted him to repeat the confession to his common-law wife, Mrs. Twila Hoffman, so her testimony should not have been admitted against him.

—His positive identification by the rape victim also followed his confession, so she should not have been permitted to testify about the identification.

In rejecting the latter contention, the Arizona Supreme Court said Miranda's trial judge, [Lawrence K.] Wren of Flagstaff, went even further than he should have by instructing jurors to disregard the victim's testimony.

Regarding Miranda's confession to Mrs. Hoffman, the Arizona Supreme Court said that she was not acting for the police.

The Court added that there was a sufficient "break in the stream of events" between his inadmissible confession to police and his confession to Mrs. Hoffman to make her testimony admissible.[59]

As far as the Arizona Supreme Court was concerned, Miranda would have to serve his sentence.

Once again, Flynn asked the U.S. Supreme Court to review the decision of the Arizona Supreme Court. His second appeal did not interest the nine justices, however, and on October 13, 1969, they declined to hear the case. For all the glory of his first Supreme Court appeal, Miranda was still behind bars with a sentence of twenty to thirty years.

Miranda's Later Life and Death

Ernesto Miranda's name became famous because of the Supreme Court decision in his case. He profited very little from his fame, though. After his retrial, he was back in the same position as before the Supreme Court decision. He was in prison with a long sentence. Over the next few years, he turned his attention to constructive pursuits. He earned a high-school

Congress Tries to Overrule *Miranda*

In 1968, Congress passed a law that made many changes in criminal procedure in federal courts. Signed into law by President Johnson, the law was officially entitled the Omnibus Crime Control and Safe Streets Act of 1968. One part of the law stated that "in any criminal prosecution brought by the United States or by the District of Columbia, a confession . . . shall be admissible in evidence if it is voluntarily given." The law further stated that the failure by police to give Miranda warnings does not mean that a confession must be suppressed in court. The giving of Miranda warnings was listed as one factor to consider in determining whether a confession was voluntarily made. The 1968 law reinstated the voluntariness rule (which had been the law prior to *Miranda*) in federal criminal cases. In essence, Congress was overruling the *Miranda* decision in the federal courts.

This new law appeared to be unconstitutional, in that the Supreme Court had decided in *Miranda* that the Fifth Amendment requires the giving of warnings and the appointment of a lawyer to advise poor suspects in custodial interrogation. In almost all federal criminal cases, the prosecution has complied with the *Miranda* ruling and ignored the easier standard of the 1968 law.

On February 8, 1999, however, the United States Court of Appeals in Richmond, Virginia, decided the case of *United States v. Dickerson*. That Court held that the 1968 law, not the *Miranda* decision, governed the admissibility of Dickerson's confession (voluntary, but without the *Miranda* warnings) in the U.S. District Court. The government did not rely on the 1968 law in *Dickerson*, but the Court of Appeals decided on its own to address the issue. There is a very good chance that the U.S. Supreme Court will agree to hear argument in the *Dickerson* case. If so, that decision could determine whether *Miranda* will remain in full effect into the new century.

---

diploma and earned some college credits through a correspondence course. He impressed a majority of his parole board and was released on parole in December of 1972. For the first time in over nine years, he was free. He was thirty years old.

Miranda returned to Mesa and lived with his stepmother and two brothers. He worked at a car recycling plant and then in a produce warehouse, making a good impression on his bosses in both jobs. He could not work as a barber, because convicted felons could not obtain a barber's license in Arizona. He had little money and became unhappy.

On July 23, 1974, the police in Tempe stopped Miranda for driving his car on the wrong side of the road. When the officer searched him and the car, he found a gun and some illegal drugs. Miranda was not convicted of charges arising from this arrest, but the possession of a gun and illegal drugs violated the conditions of his parole. He was sent back to the prison in Florence on January 16, 1975. On April 28, 1975, he was rereleased on parole, given another chance to avoid trouble in the free world.

He got a job at a tire company. To increase his income a little bit, he sold Miranda warning cards that he had personally autographed. He charged $1.50 or $2.00 for these cards.

On Saturday night, January 31, 1976, Miranda went to a bar where he drank and played cards with two other men. The men accused each other of cheating and began a violent fistfight. After the fight ended, Miranda went to the bathroom to wash blood from his hands. When he came out of the bathroom, one of the other men in the fight attacked him with a knife, stabbing him once in the stomach and once in the upper chest. An ambulance was called and took Miranda to Good Samaritan Hospital. He was dead on arrival. Although his thirty-five years of life were lived on the margins of American society, his name is still famous among police officers, lawyers, and all people interested in criminal law and civil liberties.

Notes

Chapter 1: The Crime

1. *United States Supreme Court Records and Briefs*, Record on Appeal, *Miranda v. Arizona*, Washington, DC: Congressional Information Services, 1966, p. 25.
2. Record on Appeal, *Miranda v. Arizona*, p. 32.
3. Quoted in Liva Baker, *Miranda: Crime, Law, and Politics.* New York, Atheneum, 1983, p. 5.
4. Quoted in Baker, *Miranda: Crime, Law, and Politics*, p. 12.

Chapter 2: The Interrogation and Confession

5. "Man Signs Confession," *Arizona Republic*, March 14, 1963, p. 8.
6. "Man Signs Confession," p. 8.
7. Quoted in Baker, *Miranda: Crime, Law, and Politics*, p. 12.
8. Quoted in Baker, *Miranda: Crime, Law, and Politics*, p. 13.
9. Record on Appeal, *Miranda v. Arizona*, p. 69.
10. Quoted in Baker, *Miranda: Crime, Law, and Politics*, p. 13.
11. Record on Appeal, *Miranda v. Arizona*, p. 5.
12. Quoted in Baker, *Miranda: Crime, Law, and Politics*, p. 20.
13. Record on Appeal, *Miranda v. Arizona*, p. 9.

Chapter 3: The Trial

14. Record on Appeal, *Miranda v. Arizona*, pp. 14–15.
15. Record on Appeal, *Miranda v. Arizona*, p. 16.
16. Record on Appeal, *Miranda v. Arizona*, p. 19.
17. Record on Appeal, *Miranda v. Arizona*, p. 20.
18. Record on Appeal, *Miranda v. Arizona*, p. 33.
19. Record on Appeal, *Miranda v. Arizona*, p. 35.
20. Record on Appeal, *Miranda v. Arizona*, pp. 37–38.
21. Record on Appeal, *Miranda v. Arizona*, p. 41.
22. Record on Appeal, *Miranda v. Arizona*, p. 51.
23. Record on Appeal, *Miranda v. Arizona*, p. 54.
24. Record on Appeal, *Miranda v. Arizona*, pp. 57–58.
25. Record on Appeal, *Miranda v. Arizona*, pp. 66, 63.
26. "Jury Convicts Phoenician," *Arizona Republic*, June 21, 1963, p. 9.

Chapter 4: The Appeal to the Arizona Supreme Court

27. *Arizona Reports*, vol. 98, 1965, pp. 18, 35–36.

Chapter 5: At the U.S. Supreme Court

28. Brief for Petitioner, *Miranda v. Arizona*, pp. 2–3.
29. Brief for Petitioner, *Miranda v. Arizona*, p. 47.
30. Brief of the ACLU as amicus curiae, *Miranda v. Arizona*, pp. 13–14, 23.
31. *Landmark Briefs and Arguments of the Supreme Court of the United States: Constitutional Law*, Bethesda, MD: University Publications of America, 1975, vol. 63, p. 850.
32. *Landmark Briefs and Arguments of the Supreme Court*, pp. 853–54.
33. *Landmark Briefs and Arguments of the Supreme Court*, pp. 860–861.
34. *Landmark Briefs and Arguments of the Supreme Court*, p. 862.

Chapter 6: The Supreme Court Decision

35. *United States Reports*, vol. 384, p. 439.
36. *United States Reports*, vol. 384, p. 444.
37. *United States Reports*, vol. 384, p. 444.
38. *United States Reports*, vol. 384, pp. 445, 455.
39. *United States Reports*, vol. 384, pp. 467, 468, 469.
40. *United States Reports*, vol. 384, p. 469.
41. *United States Reports*, vol. 384, p. 472.
42. *United States Reports*, vol. 384, p. 467.
43. *United States Reports*, vol. 384, p. 492.
44. *United States Reports*, vol. 384, pp. 505, 513.
45. *United States Reports*, vol. 384, pp. 515–17.
46. *United States Reports*, vol. 384, pp. 518–19, 524.
47. *United States Reports*, vol. 384, p. 526.
48. *United States Reports*, vol. 384, pp. 542–43.
49. Fred P. Graham, "High Court Puts New Curb on Powers of the Police to Interrogate Suspects," *New York Times*, June 14, 1966, p. 1.
50. John P. MacKenzie, "High Court Curbs Police Questioning," *Washington Post*, June 14, 1966, p. 1.

51. Quoted in Bernard Weinraub, "City's Police Head Fears Loss of Ability to Offer Data to Prosecutors," *New York Times*, June 15, 1966, pp. 1, 28.
52. Quoted in Baker, *Miranda: Crime, Law, and Politics*, p. 176.
53. Quoted in Jack Crowe, "Ruling Handcuffs Police," *Arizona Republic*, June 15, 1966, pp. 1, 10.
54. Quoted in Leonard Downie Jr., "Police Move to Meet New Court Ruling," *Washington Post*, June 15, 1966, pp. A1, A6.
55. Quoted in Fred P. Graham, "General Reaction Is Mild— Crime Unit Aide Sees No Major Changes," *New York Times*, June 15, 1966, pp. 1, 28.

Chapter 7: After the *Miranda* Decision

56. Quoted in Baker, *Miranda: Crime, Law, and Politics*, p. 197.
57. *Rhode Island v. Innis, United States Reports*, vol. 446, p. 304.
58. *United States Reports*, vol. 417, p. 443.
59. Bill King, "Miranda's 2nd Trial for Rape Upheld by Arizona High Court," *Arizona Republic*, February 7, 1969, pp. B1, B3.

Timeline

1941
Ernesto Miranda is born in Mesa, Arizona.

1954
Miranda is arrested for the first time for auto theft.

1958–1959
Miranda serves in the U.S. Army and receives an undesirable discharge.

1962
Miranda, Twila Hoffman, and her children move to Mesa.

March 3, 1963
Lois Ann Jameson is kidnapped and raped in Phoenix.

March 13, 1963
While in police custody, Miranda confesses to kidnapping and raping Jameson.

June 20, 1963
A jury finds Miranda guilty of kidnapping and raping Jameson.

June 27, 1963
Judge Yale McFate sentences Miranda to a prison sentence of between twenty and thirty years.

December 10, 1963
Attorney Alvin Moore submits a written brief to the Arizona Supreme Court arguing that Miranda's confession was invalid.

June 22, 1964
The U.S. Supreme Court decides the case of *Escobedo v. Illinois*, determining the suspect's right to counsel during police custodial interrogation.

April 22, 1965
The Arizona Supreme Court affirms Miranda's convictions.

November 22, 1965
The U.S. Supreme Court decides to hear Miranda's appeal.

February 28, 1966
The U.S. Supreme Court hears oral arguments in Miranda's appeal.

June 13, 1966
The Supreme Court decides that Miranda's confession was invalid and that he must receive a new trial.

February 1967
Miranda is retried in Phoenix and is again found guilty of kidnapping and raping Lois Ann Jameson in 1963.

February 6, 1969
The Arizona Supreme Court affirms Miranda's convictions.

October 13, 1969
The U.S. Supreme Court refuses to hear Miranda's appeal from his second trial and state appeal.

December 1972
Miranda is released from prison on parole.

January 31, 1976
Miranda is stabbed in a bar fight and dies.

For Further Reading

Books

Gail Blasser Riley, *Miranda v. Arizona: Rights of the Accused*. Springfield, NJ: Enslow, 1994. This readable book for young students has a strong discussion of interrogation law before *Miranda*. The author is a lawyer and a former teacher.

G. Edward White, *The American Judicial Tradition*. New York: Oxford University Press, 1976. This entertaining book gives lively histories of the most prominent appellate judges in U.S. history. One chapter is about Earl Warren and some of the justices who served with him. The author is a law professor and one of the leading legal historians in this country.

Paul B. Wice, *Miranda v. Arizona: "You Have the Right to Remain Silent . . ."*. Danbury, CT: Franklin Watts, 1996. This is another book written with young readers in mind. The author, a professor of political science, traces interrogation law all the way back to ancient Egypt and looks ahead to the impact of *Miranda* in the twenty-first century.

Newspaper Articles

Peter Carlson, "You Have the Right to Remain Silent . . .; but in the Post-Miranda Age, the Police Have Found New and Creative Ways to Make You Talk," *Washington Post*, September 13, 1998.

Robert Greiff, "Miranda—a Man of Contradictions," *Washington Post*, February 15, 1976.

Jan Hoffman, "Questioning Miranda," *New York Times*, March 29 and 30, 1998.

Works Consulted

Books

Liva Baker, *Miranda: Crime, Law, and Politics*. New York: Atheneum, 1983. This is the most complete treatment of the *Miranda* case and its effect on both the legal system and national politics.

Bruce Allen Murphy, *Fortas: The Rise and Ruin of a Supreme Court Justice*. New York: William Morrow, 1988. This biography of Abe Fortas contains a detailed discussion of his ill-fated nomination to be chief justice, doomed by the *Miranda* decision and other criminal cases decided by the Supreme Court under Earl Warren.

Bernard Schwartz, *Super Chief: Earl Warren and His Supreme Court—a Judicial Biography*. New York: New York University Press, 1983. This is a splendid history of the Supreme Court under Chief Justice Warren. *Miranda* is one of the cases discussed in detail.

Periodicals

Peter D. Baird, "The Confessions of Ernesto Arturo Miranda," *Arizona Attorney*, October 1991.

Peter D. Baird, "Miranda Memories," *Litigation*, Winter 1990.

Jack Crowe, "Ruling Handcuffs Police," *Arizona Republic*, June 15, 1966.

Leonard Downie Jr., "Police Move to Meet New Court Ruling," *Washington Post*, June 15, 1966.

Fred P. Graham, "General Reaction Is Mild—Crime Unit Aide Sees No Major Changes," *New York Times*, June 15, 1966.

Fred P. Graham, "High Court Puts New Curb on Powers of the Police to Interrogate Suspects," *New York Times*, June 14, 1966.

Lawrence Herman, "The Supreme Court, the Attorney General, and the Good Old Days of Police Interrogation," *Ohio State Law Journal*, vol. 48, Summer 1987.

"Jury Convicts Phoenician," *Arizona Republic*, June 21, 1963.

Bill King, "Miranda's 2nd Trial for Rape Upheld by Arizona High Court," *Arizona Republic*, February 7, 1969.

Susan R. Klein, "*Miranda* Deconstitutionalized: When the Self-Incrimination Clause and the Civil Rights Act Collide," *University of Pennsylvania Law Review*, vol. 143, 1994.

John P. MacKenzie, "High Court Curbs Police Questioning," *Washington Post*, June 14, 1966.

"Man Signs Confession," *Arizona Republic*, March 14, 1963.

Bernard Weinraub, "City's Police Head Fears Loss of Ability to Offer Data to Prosecutors," *New York Times*, June 15, 1966.

Legal References

Landmark Briefs and Arguments of the Supreme Court of the United States: Constitutional Law, vol. 63. Bethesda, MD: University Publications of America, 1975.

United States Supreme Court Records and Briefs. Washington, DC: Congressional Information Services, 1966. Microfiche.

Index

Picture Credits

About the Author

John Hogrogian is a lawyer who lives and works in New York City. He frequently argues appeals in the courts of New York State. This is his first book on legal history, a topic that interests him greatly. He has previously written on the history of sports, especially baseball, football, and basketball. He also loves playing softball on his office team every summer.